THE GOURMET'S GUIDE TO

COOKING WITH

WINE

First published in the United States of America by
Quarry Books, a member of
Quayside Publishing Group
100 Cummings Center
Suite 406-L
Beverly, Massachusetts 01915-6101
Telephone: (978) 282-9590
Fax: (978) 283-2742
www.quarrybooks.com

Library of Congress Cataloging-in-Publication Data
Boteler, Alison Molinare.
  The gourmet's guide to cooking with wine : how to use wine to take simple recipes
from ordinary to extraordinary / Alison Boteler.
      p. cm.
  Includes index.
  ISBN-13: 978-1-59253-470-8
  ISBN-10: 1-59253-470-8
  1. Cookery (Wine) I. Title.
  TX726.B5957 2008
  641.6'22—dc22

                                                      2008000553
                                                           CIP

ISBN-13: 978-1-59253-470-8
ISBN-10: 1-59253-470-8

10 9 8 7 6 5 4 3 2 1

Page Layout: Claire MacMaster, barefoot art graphic design
Photography: Madeline Polss
Food Styling: Dwayne Ridgaway
Technical Editing: Sandra Smith

Printed in China

THE GOURMET'S GUIDE TO
COOKING WITH

WINE

How to Use Wine to Take Simple Recipes from Ordinary to Extraordinary

BEVERLY MASSACHUSETTS

QUARRY BOOKS

ALISON BOTELER

Contents

Introduction

As a college student, I had my own radio show called *Alison's Restaurant*. One of the first guests that I interviewed was Julia Child, my childhood idol. She had a wonderful quote about cooking with wine. Julia loved to say, "If you put rot-gut in, you'll get rot-gut out." She had a good point. If you don't like the wine enough to drink it, don't pour it in your food! The cooking process will only concentrate an unappealing flavor. Conversely, a nice wine will only enhance a dish, such as in a sauce whose flavors are intensified through reduction.

In short, don't—and I repeat, don't—use "cooking wine" from the supermarket shelf for your culinary pursuits.

That's not to say that we should dip into our retirement funds to make Beef Bourguignon. There are many modestly priced wines on the market that will do the job quite nicely. Get to know your local wine merchant; let him introduce you to labels that are best suited for your recipe and your budget. Most important, find wines whose taste you enjoy—that's what counts.

Most wine lovers are interested in the endless variety of flavors and aromas available in wine. (The alcohol in wine has no flavor of its own.) These subtle differences arise from compounds called *esters*. It is these nuances of taste and aroma that make cooking with wine so exciting.

Crafting the Flavor of Wine

Three things can affect the flavor of wine: the grape varietal, the growing environment, and the wine-making process.

Each grape varietal has unique qualities, due to factors such as the amount of sugar in the grapes. The growing environment includes the climate in which the grapes were grown, the chemistry of the soil, and the microclimate—the unique sunlight pattern and

Wine Adds Character/
The Many Characters of Wine

temperature of a given hillside. The wine-making process itself creates the flavorful esters, which are by-products of fermentation.

When wine is made, the juice of the crushed grapes is either separated from the skins, as in making white wines, or left in contact with the skins, where the skins add color to the final product in a process called *maceration*. The fermentation process is driven by *Saccharomyces cerevisiae*, the same yeast that is used in making bread. As the tiny fungi live and grow in a vat of grape juice, they eat the natural sugar from the grapes and convert it to alcohol. At a particular threshold, there is too much alcohol in the wine for the yeast to continue to thrive and they die. Depending on the varietal, there may still be some sugar in the wine, which determines its sweetness.

Other processes at work add additional layers of flavor. Oxygen in the wine will combine with the alcohol to form acid, giving the wine a dry or steely quality. Some of the acid in the wine will then combine again with the alcohol to form esters. Esters are responsible for the great diversity of flavors in wine. Essences of fruits, berries, spices, honey, herbs, and butter are all the effect of different esters.

Mastering Cooking with Wine

Cooking with wine is about tapping wine's many flavors for creating sauces that fit well with a given dish. Alcohol boils at a lower temperature than water, and the cooking process concentrates the flavoring while reducing or even eliminating the alcohol. As Julia Child always preached, the concentrated sauce will be stronger in flavor than the wine it was made from. For this reason, give some thought to the selection of wine made for either a recipe in this book or an inspired, improvised dish.

If a recipe calls for a dry white wine, one might use Sauvignon Blanc. If it calls for something spicy, one could use a Gewürztraminer, Riesling, or Viognier. Cooking with a Petit Syrah or Zinfandel might be best for a hearty meat dish. Fortified wines such as sherry, port, Madeira, and Marsala are used extensively throughout this book. They are rich in flavor and a little goes a long way. Traditionally consumed as dessert wines, these naturally complement the ingredients of so many desserts.

WHAT'S IN A NAME?

Identifying wines can be confusing. Wines are named for the type of grapes in them, for the geography of their origin, or for marketing purposes.

In Europe, where wine grapes have been grown for thousands of years, wine names are derived from geographic regions. These place names are associated with distinct grape varietals and winemaking traditions. Champagne, for example, is named for a region in France (though its creation involves a unique process as well). These names are defined by law and protected by treaties.

Wines produced outside Europe are usually identified by the name of the grape varietal from which they were made. Unfortunately, there are other name categories that muddy the waters a bit. In the United States, the name "Champagne" can be given to a sparkling wine that was not produced in Champagne and does not meet its other criteria. In countries with generic naming conventions for wines, this also causes confusion.

Finally, there are many wines that have been given proprietary names for marketing purposes. White Zinfandel is a name that was originally given to rosé wine made by Sutter Home. This wine became so popular that other rosé makers appropriated it. We tend to think of the great wine regions of France and Italy when it comes to dabbling in Wine 101. However, some of the strongest wine producers today are vineyards from Australia and South Africa. In the United States, many regions outside California are now producing unique and top-quality wines.

TYPES OF WINE BY REGION (FRANCE AND ITALY)

The following chart illustrates the regions of the great wine classics.
It's helpful to know when you are preparing a traditional European dish,
even if you do end up substituting an Australian wine or American wine.

Wine Regions: France

Wine	Region	Grapes
Banyuls	Pyrenees	Grenache
Beaujolais	Burgundy	Gamay
Bordeaux	Bordeaux	Cabernet Sauvignon, Merlot
Chablis	Burgundy	Chardonnay
Champagne	Champagne	Chardonnay, Pinot Meunier, Pinot Noir
Chartreuse	Vauvert	Herbal blend in a wine base of Mediterranean grapes such as Maccabeo
Côte d'Or	Burgundy	Pinot Noir, Chardonnay
Macon	Burgundy	Pinot Blanc, Chardonnay, Gamay Noir, Pinot Noir, Pinot Gris
Medoc	Bordeaux	Cabernet Sauvignon, Merlot
Muscadet	Loire Valley	Melon de Bourgogne
Sancerre	Loire Valley	Sauvignon Blanc, Pinot Noir
Sauternes	Bordeaux	Semillon, Cabernet, Muscadelle
Vouvray	Loire Valley	Chenin Blanc

Wine Regions: Italy

Wine	Region	Grapes
Amarone	Venice	Corvina Veronese, Rondinella, Molinara
Asti Spumanti	Turin	Muscat
Barolo	Piedmont	Nebbiolo
Castel del Monte	Apulia	Uva di Troia, Pinot Noir, Sangiovese, Montepulciano, Aglianico
Chianti	Tuscany	Sangiovese, Canaiolo, Trebbiano, Malvasia
Est! Est!! Est!!!	Tuscany	Trebbiano and Malvasia
Gavi	Piedmont	Cortese
Marsala	Sicily	Grillo, Catarratto, Inzolia, Damaschino, Pignatello, Calabrese, Nerello, Mascalese, Nero d'Avola
Montepulciano d'Abruzzo	Abruzzi	Montepulciano
Soave	Venice	Garganega, Trebbiano di Soave
Valpolicella	Venice	Corvina, Molinara, Rondinella

TYPES OF WINE BY GRAPE VARIETAL

The section that follows lists the major types of wine by grape varietal. Fortified, dessert, and "other" types of wines are not named for their varietal grapes used since these wines have historically been identified by other names. Blended wines are identified by the predominant wine in the blend, which in many places is dictated by laws that regulate the percentage of blended wines allowed. Even within varietal categories, factors such as terroir and wine-making methods affect the flavor of wine produced. For each varietal the characteristic flavors are shown along with a short biography.

Red Wines

Barbera
Berrylike flavors
Where grown: Italy, California, Slovenia
About: Barbera originated in the Piedmont region of Italy. This is the second-most-planted grape in Italy and is widely used to make table wine. The grape is very acidic and produces an acidic tang.

Cabernet Sauvignon
Black currant flavor
Where grown: France, California, Australia, and Chile
About: Cabernet Sauvignon is responsible for the great red wines of France's Medoc region.

Chianti
Floral taste, complex
Where grown: Italy (Tuscany)
About: Originates from the areas around Florence and Sienna in Italy. Chianti is derived mainly from the Sangiovese grapes but may also contain Cabernet Sauvignon.

Gamay
Raspberry, floral flavors
Where grown: France (Beaujolais region), California, and Canada
About: This grape is used to make Beaujolais Nouveau. The grapes are hand-harvested and fermentation occurs inside the grape where individual berries trap the forming carbon dioxide bubbles until they burst.

Merlot
Dry with cherry, plum flavors
Where grown: France, Italy, California, Oregon, and Washington
About: Originated in France's Bordeaux region, where it is the predominant grape. It is added to Bordeaux blends to give body and softness.

Nebbiolo
Raspberry, plum, rose flavors
Where grown: Italy (Piedmont)
About: Used to make Barolo wine. *Nebbiolo* is Italian for "fog" and refers to the thick fogs that hang over the growing region in October. Flavors are complex and contain bitter tannins. It is aged for three to five years to alleviate the tannic taste.

Petite Syrah
Peppery, complex flavor
Where grown: California
About: Mainly grown in California, this varietal is used both to make stand-alone wines and for blending.

Pinot Noir
Black cherry, complex flavor
Where grown: France, California, and Oregon
About: Pinot Noir is an ancient varietal. It is most famous for its contribution to the wines of France's Burgundy region.

Sangiovese
Cherry, spice flavors
Where grown: Italy
About: Originating in Italy's Tuscany region, Sangiovese is the main varietal used to make Chianti wine. It is increasingly grown outside of Italy.

Syrah/Shiraz
Dry wines with black cherry, roasted pepper, spice flavors
Where grown: France, Australia, South Africa, and California
About: Thought to have been brought from Iran, Shiraz is the main grape varietal in France's Rhone Valley. It is frequently blended.

Tempranillo
Cherry, spice, tobacco flavors
Where grown: Spain
About: Originating in Spain, Tempranillo was brought to the New World by Spanish conquistadores. It is beginning to enjoy wider popularity outside its homelands.

Zinfandel
Spice flavors
Where grown: California
About: Was brought to America from a specimen in the Imperial State Nursery in Vienna in the 1820s. Today Zinfandel is used to make a wide variety of wines, including sweet White Zinfandels, light-bodied reds, full-bodied dry reds, and sweet dessert wines.

White Wines

Chablis
Dry, steely
Where grown: France (Burgundy)
About: Originating in France's Burgundy area near the town of Chablis, it is made from the Chardonnay grape.

Chardonnay
Fig, peach, honey, spice flavors
Where grown: France (Burgundy), Australia, and California
About: Often blended with other wines, Chardonnay is an important ingredient in Chablis and Champagne.

Chenin Blanc
Pear, peach, grape, honey flavors (ranges dry to sweet and fruity)
Where grown: France (Loire Valley)
About: Originating in France's Anjou region, Chenin Blanc is used to make dessert and sparkling wines.

Gewürztraminer
Fruit, flower, nut flavors (ranges from dry to slightly sweet)
Where grown: France (Alsace), Germany, Italy, Australia, and the United States
About: Originating in the Tyrolean Alps, Gewürztraminer is named for the town of Tramin, Italy. This grape is naturally high in sugar.

Muscat
Sweet (ranges from light to heavily sweet)
Where grown: Italy, France, California, Oregon, and Australia
About: Originating in Spain and Portugal, Muscat grapes are used to make Muscatel wine as well as Sherry.

Pinot Blanc
Dry wine with apple and spice flavors
Where grown: France (Alsace), Germany, Hungary, and California
About: Originating in France's Alsace region, this grape is used to produce wine that varies from dry to sweet.

Pinot Gris
Dry wine with subtle hints of almonds, peaches
Where grown: France (Alsace), Italy

About: Originating in France's Burgundy region, this grape is used to produce wines of greatly varying style depending on the production area.

Riesling

Balanced wines ranging from dry to sweet. Floral, fruit flavors
Where grown: Germany, France (Alsace)
About: Originating in Germany's Rhine Valley, Riesling grapes are used to make both dry and off-dry wines. The off-dry wines are made by late harvesting of the grapes. Riesling is very acidic, making it age well (often in barrels for more than one hundred years).

Sauvignon/Fumé Blanc

Dry wines with herby, grassy flavors
Where grown: France, California, New Zealand, and Italy
About: Originating in France's Bordeaux region, Sauvignon Blanc grapes are used to make wine in a variety of styles, from dry Pouilly-Fumé to sweet dessert wines such as Sauterne.

Semillon

Ranges from dry to sweet
Where grown: France (Bordeaux), Australia, Chile, South Africa, and Washington State
About: Grown widely throughout the world, Semillon grapes are often blended with other wines such as Chardonnay or Sauvignon Blanc. It helps to round out the dry whites. When it is used to sweeten the off-dry whites, such as Sauternes, it becomes the dominant ingredient.

Viognier

Dry wines with peach or apricot flavors
Where grown: France (Rhône Valley) and California
About: Viognier is a rare varietal with most cultivation occurring in the Rhône Valley. Compounds called terpenes give Viognier its flowery aroma.

Dessert and Fortified Wines
Madeira

Sweet, nutty flavors
Where produced: Portugal (Madeira Islands)
About: Originally this Portuguese wine was shipped in wooden barrels, often making long sea voyages. As with other fortified wines, additional ethyl alcohol "spirits" were added as a preservative. Today, storage in special heated buildings called *estufas* simulates the historical long voyages through tropical waters. Madeira was the wine most frequently enjoyed by early American colonists as no other wines were available in the English colonies.

Marsala

Sweet, fruity flavors
Where produced: Italy (Sicily)
About: Marsala wine is named for the Italian city of Marsala. It is widely used for cooking in Italian restaurants.

Port

Sweet, nutty, fruity, spicy flavors
Where produced: Portugal (Douro River Valley)
About: This sweet dessert wine is fortified with "spirits" and aged in bottles or in wooden barrels in caves. Ports aged in bottles are not exposed to the air and differ in their characteristics from those aged in barrels.

Sherry
Sweet, nutty flavors
Where produced: Spain (Jerez area)
About: Sherry is a fortified wine made by adding brandy after fermentation is complete. Sherry is naturally dry and any sweetness is added after fermentation.

Vermouth
Ranges from dry to sweet with herby, spicy flavors
Where produced: Italy, France
About: This Italian wine is made with a proprietary blend of herbs and spices. Generally, Italian vermouths are thought of as white vermouths, and French vermouths as red vermouths, though this is not always the case. The sweeter red vermouths are enjoyed as dessert wines and used in drinks such as the Manhattan. Dry white vermouths are used for martinis.

Other Wines
Champagne/Sparkling Wines
Tart, fruity flavors
Where produced: France (Champagne region), and worldwide for other sparkling wines
About: Champagne is a sparkling wine named for France's Champagne region and produced by the *méthode champenoise*, which is protected by law and treaty. Like other sparkling wines, it contains carbon dioxide, which slowly bubbles off after opening. Champagne is made mainly with Chardonnay, or the black Pinot Noir or Pinot Meunier grapes.

Kosher Wine
Traditionally sweet, but comes in all styles
Where produced: worldwide
About: The category of kosher wine includes any wine considered kosher under Jewish religious law, the definition of which varies between Orthodox and non-Orthodox interpretations. In the past, extremely sweet wines were associated with the kosher category, but this is no longer the case and a great variety now exist.

Rosé
Tart, fruity flavor
Where produced: France, California, and Australia
About: Any wine that is slightly colored by the grape juice's contact with the grape skins (but without the long contact that produces red wines) is considered rosé wine. Rosé wines were traditionally dry, but many sweet rosés were produced for the mass market after World War II. This is now changing again, with many dry rosés available.

White Zinfandel
Sweet, fruity flavors
Where produced: California
About: The original White Zinfandel was made by Sutter Home winery and was an accident. The sweet rosé wine that resulted was so popular that it was copied by other wineries, who borrowed the name for their products.

Retsina
Pine resin flavors
Where produced: Greece, Cyprus

About: The story has it that when the Romans invaded Greece, the Greeks put all their wine in pine barrels so that the conquerors would not like the taste of it. Whether this is true or just a patriotic legend, Retsina is a unique, flavorful wine.

Verjus
Sour flavors
Where produced: France
About: Verjus is a sour-tasting drink made from unripe grapes, sometimes with the addition of herbs and spices. It is used in French cuisine for making sauces and salad dressing and for deglazing.

Sake
Tropical spices, mineral, coconut flavors
Where produced: Japan, China, Southeast Asia, North America, South America, and Australia
About: Sake is rice wine. It is made in a double-brewing process in which mold is used to convert the rice to sugar, and yeast is then added to turn the sugar into alcohol. Sake is an important part of Shinto purification rituals and is also used in the Japanese tea ceremony.

Mirin
Sweet (used in Teriyaki sauce)
Where produced: Japan
About: Mirin is a rice wine similar to sake but with a lower alcohol content. It is sometimes served with sushi and is an important ingredient in teriyaki sauce.

Wine in the Kitchen

When it comes to stocking a wine pantry, affordable bottles that will pair well with a variety of foods should be kept on hand. Nearly 75 percent of all red and white wines are considered "dry." For that reason, many of the recipes in this book simply refer to using "dry red" or "dry white" wine. Many sweeter white wines are referred to as "off dry." Fortified wines such as sherry, port (one of the few sweet reds), Marsala, and Madeira will always come in handy. Sherry is the most common wine used in cooking. For Asian dishes, be sure to have a bottle of mirin.

The most common cooking technique using wine involves either braising or deglazing a pan. It's here where creativity can come through. Most recipes involving liquids or broth can be adjusted so wine is a key ingredient and flavor enhancer. This is especially true when making original sauces. Also, wine is an excellent poaching liquid for fresh fruits. Baking with wine usually involves adding modest amounts of a sweet, fortified wine (such as sherry or port) as a flavoring.

The following list suggests some of the most useful wines to keep on hand for your everyday cooking repertoire. Always try to have one or two wines from the dry red, dry white, and off-dry white categories on the shelf along with a complete selection of fortified wines.

Dry Red Wines
Cabernet Sauvignon
Merlot
Nebbiolo
Petite Syrah
Pinot Noir
Sangiovese
Syrah/Shiraz
Tempranillo

Dry White Wines
Chablis
Chardonnay
Pinot Blanc
Pinot Gris
Sauvignon/Fumé Blanc
Viognier

Off-Dry White Wines
Gewürztraminer
Muscat
Semillon

Fortified Wines
Madeira
Marsala
Port
Sherry
Vermouth

Other Wines
Kosher or fruit-based wine
Mirin

ALCOHOL BURN-OFF
In all cooking techniques with wine, most of the alcohol burns off. This makes cooking with wine an ideal way to enhance dishes without adding calories. The table below shows the amount of alcohol that burns off during cooking.

Alcohol Burn-off

Preparation Technique/Cooking Time	% Alcohol Retained
Simmered, baked, braised, or roasted:	
2.5 hours	5%
2 hours	10%
1.5 hours	20%
1 hour	25%
30 minutes	35%
15 minutes	40%
Alcohol added to an uncooked dish and stored overnight	70%
Alcohol flambéed in a skillet or chafing dish	75%
Alcohol added to boiling liquid or sauce, then removed from heat	85%

Appetizers and Soups

Blue Cheese Dip with Roasted Pecans

The rich character of roasted pecans plays well against the pungent flavor of blue cheese. The dip pairs well with the mild bitterness of endive leaves, or celery sticks and flatbread.

1   package (8 ounces, or 225 g) cream cheese, softened
3   tablespoons (45 ml) vermouth
1   cup (120 g) crumbled blue cheese
½   cup (115 g) mayonnaise
2   teaspoons (10 ml) Worcestershire sauce
1   cup (100 g) toasted pecans*
    Endive leaves or celery sticks
    Flatbread crackers

Beat cream cheese until smooth. Blend in vermouth, blue cheese, mayonnaise, Worcestershire sauce, and toasted pecans. Chill until ready to use and serve in a bowl surrounded by endive or celery and flatbread.

*For toasted pecans: Preheat oven to 350°F (180°C, or gas mark 4) and spread pecans on a baking sheet. Bake for 6 to 8 minutes, stirring once or twice, until evenly golden brown. Watch carefully to avoid burning.

Prep = 15 minutes   **Cook** = 5 minutes (for toasting pecans)
Yield = 2½ cups

Burgundy and Berry Glazed Meatballs

Take advantage of ready-made meatballs in the grocer's freezer section for creative party appetizers. Prebaking meatballs before simmering them in a slow cooker draws off additional fat.

- 2 packages (16 ounces, or 455 g, each) frozen meatballs, thawed
- ½ cup (120 ml) Burgundy or red wine
- ½ cup (125 g) cranberry-orange sauce
- ½ teaspoon dried mustard
- ½ teaspoon ground ginger
- 1 bottle (12 ounces, or 355 ml) chili sauce

Preheat oven to 350°F (180°C, or gas mark 4). Arrange meatballs on a 11 × 15-inch (27.5 × 37.5-cm) baking sheet and bake for 10 minutes, until fat starts to cook off of meatballs. Combine red wine, cranberry-orange sauce, mustard, ginger, and bottle of chili sauce in a slow cooker. Add meatballs. Cover and cook on low setting for 2 to 3 hours, until sauce is like a glaze.

Serve immediately in a chafing dish.

Prep = 12 minutes   **Cook** = 2 to 3 hours
Yield = 12 to 16 servings

Cranberry and Port-Glazed Brie

This holiday favorite is simple to create.
Plates, saucepan lids, and glassware can be used
as templates for cutting pastry rounds.

- 1 sheet of frozen puff pastry (from a 17.3-ounce [484.4-g] package), thawed
- 1 round (14 to 15 ounces, or 400 to 420 g) Brie cheese
- 1 large egg, beaten
- Assorted crackers

FOR CRANBERRY-PORT WINE GLAZE:
- 1 cup (95 g) fresh cranberries
- ⅓ cup (75 g) firmly packed brown sugar
- 3 tablespoons (45 ml) port

Heat oven to 400°F (200°C, or gas mark 6). Spray a baking sheet with nonstick cooking spray. Roll pastry out on a lightly floured surface until it measures 9 × 16 inches (22.5 × 40-cm). Cut out an 8½-inch (21-cm) circle and a 7-inch (17.5-cm) circle.

To make Cranberry Port Wine Glaze: In a medium saucepan, combine cranberries, brown sugar, and port. Heat to boiling, stirring frequently. Reduce heat and simmer, uncovered, for 15 to 20 minutes, stirring frequently, until cranberries are very tender and sauce is thick. Chill for several hours or overnight.

Place Brie round in the center of the 8½-inch (21-cm) circle. Spoon cranberry glaze over cheese. Bring pastry up and press around the side of cheese. Brush sides of pastry with egg and cover with 7-inch (17.5-cm) circle, pressing around edge to seal. Glaze top and sides of pastry with egg. Cut out decorations from remaining pastry scraps to arrange on top; brush with egg and place on cookie sheet. Bake for 20 to 25 minutes, until golden brown. Cool on baking sheet for 30 minutes before removing. Serve on a platter with crackers.

Prep = 20 minutes   **Cook** = 20 to 25 minutes   **Yield** = 12 servings

Italian Sautéed Olives with Vermouth

This elevates olives to stand-alone
status on any antipasto or wine-and-cheese tray.
Warm, wine-infused olives are popular at most gatherings
and will please most palates.

- 2 tablespoons (28 ml) extra-virgin olive oil
- 2 tablespoons (8 g) chopped fresh parsley
- 2 scallions, thinly sliced
- 2 cloves garlic, crushed
- ½ teaspoon crushed red pepper flakes
- 1 jar (8 ounces, or 225 g) kalamata olives, drained and pitted
- 1 jar (8 ounces, or 225 g) Greek green olives, drained and pitted
- 1 jar (8 ounces, or 225 g) Gaeta olives, drained and pitted
- ¼ cup (60 ml) dry vermouth
  Sliced French baguette and assorted cheese wedges
  (such as Asiago, Gouda, Manchego, and Brie)

In a medium skillet, heat olive oil and sauté parsley, scallions, garlic, and red pepper flakes for about 4 minutes. Stir in olives and vermouth. Cover and simmer for about 5 minutes, shaking the pan so that olives don't stick. Remove cover and continue cooking for 2 more minutes or until liquid has evaporated. Serve warm or at room temperature, with bread and assorted cheeses.

Prep = 10 minutes   **Cook** = 11 minutes
Yield = 12 to 16 servings

Hot Crab and Artichoke Dip Chablis

This dip is wickedly rich, but it's always a real hit.
Most like it piping hot, but it is equally delicious when
served cold the next day . . . that is, if there are
any leftovers!

1 package (8 ounces, or 225 g) cream cheese, softened
1 clove garlic, crushed
¼ cup (25 g) grated Parmesan cheese
1 cup (115 g) grated Monterey Jack cheese
½ teaspoon Worcestershire sauce
½ cup (120 ml) Chablis or white wine
⅔ cup (150 g) mayonnaise
1 can (14 ounces, or 400 g) artichoke hearts, drained well and patted dry
1 can (6 ounces, or 170 g) crabmeat, drained, cartilage removed, and flaked
4 scallions, thinly sliced
⅓ cup (32 g) sliced almonds
   Assorted crackers, celery sticks, and endive leaves

Preheat oven to 375°F (190°C, or gas mark 5). Blend cream cheese with mixer until smooth. Blend in garlic, Parmesan cheese, half of the Monterey Jack cheese, and the Worcestershire sauce, wine, and mayonnaise.

Chop up the artichokes and stir into cheese mixture along with crabmeat and scallions. Spread dip into a 9-inch (22.5-cm) glass pie plate. Sprinkle with remaining Monterey Jack cheese and almonds. Bake, uncovered for 15 to 20 minutes, or until bubbly and hot and almonds start to brown. Serve at once with crackers, celery, and endive.

Prep = 15 minutes **Cook** = 15 to 20 minutes
Yield = 12 to 16 servings

Gorgonzola and Toasted Walnut Spread with Madeira

This spread can also be shaped into cheese balls or logs for holiday gifts. Simply reserve the walnuts instead of mixing them in. Chill the cheese mixture, shape into balls or logs, and roll in walnuts as a coating.

1 cup (120 g) crumbled Gorgonzola cheese
1 package (8 ounces, or 225 g) cream cheese, softened
2 tablespoons (28 ml) heavy cream
2 tablespoons (28 ml) Madeira wine
¼ teaspoon black pepper
1 cup (150 g) toasted chopped walnuts*
1 tablespoon (4 g) chopped fresh parsley
Apple and pear slices
Sliced French bread, toasted

Combine Gorgonzola cheese, cream cheese, heavy cream, Madeira, and pepper in the bowl of a food processor. Process just until blended. Reserve 2 tablespoons (20 g) walnuts for garnish. Stir parsley and remaining walnuts into cheese. Spoon into serving dish and sprinkle with remaining walnuts. Serve with apple and pear slices along with toasted French bread.

*For toasted walnuts: Preheat oven to 350°F (180°C, or gas mark 4) and spread walnuts on a baking sheet. Bake for 6 to 8 minutes, stirring once or twice, until evenly golden brown. Watch carefully to avoid burning.

Prep = 15 minutes   **Cook** = 6 to 8 minutes (for toasting walnuts)
Yield = 12 servings

Sausage and Sherry Cheese Balls with Jezebel Sauce

Jezebel is a pineapple sauce and a popular Southern cocktail party appetizer. This version, though zesty, isn't quite as hot as the traditional preparation.

- 3   cups (360 g) biscuit baking mix
- 1   pound (455 g) bulk pork sausage
- 4   cups (about 1 pound, or 455 g) grated Cheddar cheese
- ½   cup (50 g) grated Parmesan cheese
- ¼   cup (60 ml) half-and-half
- ¼   cup (60 ml) Oloroso sherry
- ½   cup (26 g) dried rosemary leaves, crushed
- 1 ½   teaspoons chopped fresh parsley

FOR JEZEBEL SAUCE:
- 1   jar (8 ounces, or 225 g) pineapple preserves
- 1   tablespoon (15 g) prepared horseradish
- 1   teaspoon dry mustard
- 2   tablespoons (28 ml) Oloroso sherry

Preheat oven to 350°F (180°C, or gas mark 4) and spray a 10 × 15-inch (25 × 37.5-cm) jelly-roll pan with nonstick cooking spray. In a large mixing bowl, combine baking mix, sausage, Cheddar and Parmesan cheeses, half-and-half, sherry, rosemary, and parsley, until moistened. Shape into 1-inch (2.5-cm) balls and arrange on pan. Bake, uncovered, for 20 to 25 minutes or until browned. Serve warm with Jezebel Sauce.

To make Jezebel Sauce: Combine ingredients in a saucepan. Bring to a boil. Boil 1 minute and cool to room temperature.

Prep = 20 minutes   **Cook** = 20 to 25 minutes
Yield = 12 to 16 servings

Chablis Vichyssoise

Vichyssoise is an old-fashioned favorite that
is subtly seasoned only with celery and parsley. To give
it a kick, spike it with Chablis. Why not? It's totally
in keeping with its French heritage.

6	medium potatoes, peeled and diced
3	celery stalks, sliced
8	medium onions, sliced
½	cup (30 g) minced fresh parsley
1	teaspoon salt
½	teaspoon pepper
2	cups (475 ml) chicken stock
2	cups (475 ml) Chablis
1	cup (240 ml) water
1 ½	cups (355 ml) heavy cream
	Minced fresh chives

In a large stockpot, combine all of the ingredients except heavy cream and minced chives and bring to a boil. Cover and simmer for 40 minutes, or until tender. Cool and purée soup in blender in several batches. Blend in heavy cream and adjust flavor with salt and pepper. Chill for at least 4 hours or overnight. Serve in cups, sprinkled with chives.

Prep = 30 minutes   **Cook** = 40 minutes
Yield = 8 servings

Mirin-Glazed Chicken Wings

Mirin, the Japanese wine, is a popular glaze for salmon in many restaurants. Adding it to chicken wings achieves a similar result. It's important to turn the wings throughout the baking process so they achieve a rich, even, mahogany glaze.

½ cup (160 g) ginger preserves
½ cup (120 ml) pineapple juice
½ cup (120 ml) mirin
½ cup (120 g) ketchup
¼ cup (85 g) honey
¼ cup (60 g) firmly packed brown sugar
¼ cup (60 ml) teriyaki marinade
2 cloves garlic, crushed
24 chicken wing drummettes

Preheat oven to 350°F (180°C, or gas mark 4) and line a 9 × 13-inch (22.5 × 32.5-cm) baking pan with foil. Heat ginger preserves, pineapple juice, mirin, ketchup, honey, brown sugar, teriyaki marinade, and garlic in a medium saucepan. Boil 2 minutes and remove from heat. Arrange chicken in foil-lined pan and pour sauce over chicken. Bake, uncovered, for about 1 hour, turning three times while baking. Serve warm.

Prep = 15 minutes   **Cook** = 1 hour   **Yield** = 12 servings

French Onion Soup Chardonnay

First the onions are caramelized in the oven in a roasting pan, then the pan is transferred to the stove top. This novel production is well worth the effort.

- 4 tablespoons (55 g) butter
- 1 tablespoon (15 g) firmly packed brown sugar
- 1 teaspoon (5 ml) Worcestershire Sauce
- 2 large onions, sliced
- 2 cans (10½ ounces, or 315 ml, each) condensed beef broth
- 2 cups (475 ml) Chardonnay or white wine

FOR PARMESAN CROUTONS:
- 2 cups (80 g) French bread cubes
- 4 tablespoons (55 g) butter, melted
- ¼ cup (25 g) grated Parmesan cheese

- 1 cup (about 4 ounces, or 115 g) shredded Swiss cheese

Preheat oven to 325°F (170°C, or gas mark 3). In a 4-quart (3.8-L) ovenproof Dutch oven, melt butter over medium heat, stir in brown sugar, Worcestershire sauce, and onions. Bake, uncovered, for 2½ hours, stirring every 30 minutes, until onions are a deep golden brown. Remove from oven, stir in broth and wine. Heat on stove top burner to boiling.

To make Parmesan Croutons: Preheat oven to 400°F (200°C, or gas mark 6). Toss bread with butter and cheese. Spread into a 9 × 13-inch (22.5 × 32.5-cm) baking pan. Bake for 10 to 15 minutes, stirring twice, until golden brown and toasty (be careful not to burn).
   Preheat broiler. Divide soup among 6 ovenproof crocks or bowls. Top with Parmesan Croutons and Swiss cheese. Run soup bowls under broiler and heat just until glazed.

Prep = 25 minutes   **Cook** = 3 hours
Yield = 6 servings

Portobello Mushroom Caps with Crabmeat and Marsala

Stuffed mushroom caps can be served as a first course, and they are ideal for potluck occasions.

16 ounces (455 g) crabmeat, picked over to remove cartilage
½ cup (80 g) minced Vidalia onion
2 tablespoons (8 g) minced fresh parsley
1 teaspoon garlic powder
½ teaspoon dry mustard
½ teaspoon salt
2 tablespoons (28 ml) lemon juice
1 tablespoon (15 ml) Worcestershire sauce
½ cup (115 g) mayonnaise
¼ cup (60 ml) heavy cream
1 cup (120 g) herb-seasoned stuffing mix, crushed to course crumbs
1 ½ cups (150 g) grated Asiago cheese
½ cup (50 g) grated Parmesan cheese
8 portobello mushroom caps
   Paprika
⅓ cup (80 ml) Marsala

Combine crabmeat, onion, parsley, garlic powder, dry mustard, salt, lemon juice, Worcestershire sauce, mayonnaise, heavy cream, stuffing, 1 cup Asiago cheese, and ¼ cup Parmesan cheese in mixing bowl. Chill for at least 4 hours or overnight.

Preheat oven to 400°F (200°C, or gas mark 6). Brush mushroom caps and rub lightly with olive oil. Place in a 9 × 13-inch (22.5 × 32.5-cm) baking dish (tops of caps facing down). Spoon stuffing into caps. Sprinkle with remaining ½ cup (50 g) Asiago cheese, ¼ cup (25 g) Parmesan cheese, and paprika. Pour Marsala around the sides of the mushroom caps (not over stuffing). Bake for 25 to 30 minutes, until topping is golden and mushrooms are thoroughly cooked.

Prep = 10 minutes   **Cook** = 25 to 30 minutes
Yield = 4 to 8 servings

Portobello-Parmesean Bruschetta

Mushrooms can be sautéed a day ahead
and refrigerated and the appetizer assembled just
before serving. Cremini or porcini mushrooms
work just as well, as they are chopped
before sautéing.

- 2 tablespoons (28 ml) extra-virgin olive oil
- 2 cloves garlic, crushed
- 2 packages (12 ounces, or 340 g, each) portobello mushrooms, chopped
- ¼ teaspoon salt
- ⅛ teaspoon pepper
- ¼ cup (60 ml) Marsala wine
- 12 French baguette slices, ½ inch (1.25 cm) thick
- 1 cup (80 g) shredded Parmesan cheese (Do not use dry type from a canister.)

In a medium skillet over medium heat combine olive oil, garlic, and mushrooms. Sprinkle with salt and pepper. Cook, stirring occasionally, until tender and most of the moisture has evaporated (about 10 minutes). Add Marsala and continue cooking until mixture is fairly dry and liquid has evaporated.

Preheat oven to 450°F (230°C, or gas mark 8). Arrange baguette slices on baking sheet. Spoon mushroom mixture on top of each and sprinkle with cheese. Bake for 6 to 8 minutes, until edges are golden brown.

Prep = 10 minutes   **Cook** = 18 to 20 minutes   **Yield** = 12 servings

Chianti Gazpacho

This recipe came from Mary Beth Doughty
of Arlington, Virginia. In addition to Chianti, grilled
Vidalia onions enhance this version of gazpacho. If there
is no grill in the kitchen, the onions can be prepared
using a simple grilling technique in the oven
or even a toaster oven.

1   can (46 ounces, or 1.4 L) spicy vegetable juice cocktail
2   tablespoons (28 ml) extra-virgin olive oil
1   tablespoon (15 ml) red wine vinegar
¼   cup (60 ml) Chianti
1   tablespoon (4 g) minced fresh Italian parsley
1   tablespoon (4 g) minced fresh cilantro
1   tablespoon (4 g) minced fresh basil
1   cup (135 g) peeled, diced English cucumber
1   cup (180 g) seeded, diced fresh tomato or drained canned
     tomatoes
1   cup (120 g) diced celery
2   medium Vidalia onions, grilled,* then chopped
     Salt and pepper
     Sour cream and fresh chives for garnish

Combine vegetable juice cocktail, olive oil, vinegar, Chianti, parsley,
cilantro, basil, cucumber, tomato, celery, and grilled Vidalia onions.
Season with salt and pepper to taste. Chill overnight. Serve in cups
garnished with dollops of sour cream and chives. If desired, serve
with grilled shrimp on the side of the cup.

*To grill onions in oven: Preheat oven to 425°F (220°C, or gas
mark 7). Slice onions ¾ inch (1.9 cm) thick. Line a baking sheet
with nonstick aluminum foil. Spray foil with garlic-flavored cooking
oil spray. Arrange onion slices on foil and bake for 10 to 12 minutes, until undersides of onion slices have browned. Cool.

Prep = 15 minutes   **Cook** = 10 to 12 minutes   **Yield** = 8 servings

Winter Squash Soup
with Madeira

Butternut squash soup is a favorite in the autumn months. This hearty recipe nearly tends to itself in the slow cooker. For added ease, pierce the whole squash all over and microwave on high for 4 minutes. Cool and peel.

2	tablespoons (28 g) butter
1	medium onion, chopped
1	butternut squash (about 2 pounds, or 905 g), peeled and cubed
1 ½	cups (355 ml) chicken stock
½	cup Madeira
½	teaspoon dried marjoram leaves
¼	teaspoon ground black pepper
3	vegetarian vegetable bouillon cubes
1	package (8 ounces, or 225 g) cream cheese, cubed
½	cup (50 g) toasted pecans*

In a medium skillet, melt butter and sauté onion until tender. In a slow cooker, combine onion, squash, chicken stock, Madeira, marjoram, pepper, and bouillon cubes. Cover and cook over low heat for 6 to 8 hours.

In blender or food processor, purée soup mixture in thirds and return to slow cooker. Add cream cheese and blend with wire whisk. Cover and continue cooking over low heat for about 30 minutes, blending occasionally with wire whisk until soup is smooth. Serve in bowls topped with toasted pecans.

*For toasted pecans: Preheat oven to 350°F (180°C, or gas mark 4) and spread pecans on a baking sheet. Bake for 6 to 8 minutes, stirring once or twice, until evenly golden brown. Watch carefully to avoid burning.

Prep = 25 minutes   **Cook** = 6 to 8 hours   **Yield** = 8 servings

Mushroom Gratin Oloroso

Oloroso sherry matures through exposure
to air, not in a sealed barrel. This process gives it a
rich, deep color and character, making it a great accent
to woodsy cremini mushrooms. Consider serving
this dish in individual crocks.

3	tablespoons (45 g) butter
⅓	cup (55 g) minced shallots
2	cloves garlic, crushed
8	ounces (225 g) cremini mushrooms, quartered
¼	teaspoon salt
½	cup (120 ml) Oloroso sherry
¾	cup (175 ml) cream
1	tablespoon (4 g) minced fresh parsley
1	cup (about 2 ounces, or 55 g) grated Manchego cheese
1	loaf crusty French bread or crostini toasts

In a medium skillet over medium heat, melt butter. Sauté shallots and garlic in butter, stirring for about 5 minutes or until soft. Add mushrooms, sprinkle with salt, and continue cooking and stirring until most of the moisture from the mushrooms has evaporated.

Add sherry and increase heat to medium-high. Cook for about 3 minutes, or until sherry is reduced by half. Add cream and parsley. Boil for 4 to 5 minutes, until sauce is reduced to one-third its volume and coats the mushrooms.

Preheat broiler. Spoon mushrooms into a 1-quart (945-ml) ceramic crock or casserole. Top with cheese and broil, 6 inches (15 cm) from heat, for about 2 minutes or until golden and bubbling. Serve with French bread or crostini toasts.

Prep = 10 minutes   **Cook** = 25 minutes   **Yield** = 4 servings

Camembert with Cabernet Rhubarb-Cherry Chutney

Rhubarb is a delightfully tart vegetable
that is usually paired with a fruit to temper its acidity.
It is elegant in a chutney appetizer, but can also be served
alongside poultry and pork dishes.

½ cup (60 g) dried cherries
½ cup (120 ml) Cabernet Sauvignon
2 tablespoons (30 ml) balsamic vinegar
½ cup (100 g) sugar
2 cups (200 g) sliced rhubarb
¼ cup (80 g) red currant jelly
1 tablespoon (14 g) butter
½ cup (45 g) sliced almonds
1 14 ounce (14-ounce, or 400 g) round of Camembert
English stone-ground wheat crackers

Combine cherries, wine, vinegar, sugar, and rhubarb in a
saucepan. Cover and bring to a boil over high heat. Reduce
heat to low and cook, uncovered, until liquid is thick and syrupy
and rhubarb is tender. Stir in red currant jelly. Cool to room
temperature.

Melt 1 tablespoon (14 g) butter in a small skillet and sauté
almonds, stirring constantly until golden brown. Spread chutney
over cheese, and top with almonds. Serve with crackers.

Prep = 10 minutes **Cook** = 45 to 55 minutes **Yield** = 8 to 12 servings

Salad Dressings
and Salads

Alison's
House Dressing

Just as in a restaurant, a favorite house
dressing keeps dinner guests coming back for more.
This recipe originated in a favorite lunch spot, long ago.
One day, after years of pleading with the chef to divulge it,
he walked past the table and handed over a cocktail
napkin with the recipe scribbled on it. The dressing
is wonderful hot over spinach salad with apples;
Boston lettuce with bacon, egg, and tomato;
or even potato salad.

¼ cup (55 g) bacon drippings
¼ cup (60 ml) canola or vegetable oil
½ cup (80 g) chopped onions
½ cup (120 ml) cider vinegar
½ cup (100 g) sugar
¼ cup (60 ml) sherry
1 cup (225 g) mayonnaise
2 tablespoons (10 g) crumbled crisp bacon

Combine bacon drippings and oil in a medium saucepan. Add
onions and cook until soft and moisture has "sweated off."
Remove from heat and stir in vinegar and sugar. Add sherry and
return to stove, heating through until bubbling again. Remove
from heat, blend in mayonnaise and bacon. Serve immediately or
save in a jar in the refrigerator and reheat as needed.

Prep = 10 minutes   **Cook** = 10 minutes
Yield = about 2½ cups (565 g)

Caesar Salad Vermouth

No two versions of Caesar salad dressing are
exactly alike. Originally, Caesar salad was prepared
at tableside in fine restaurants with a coddled egg.
When the dressing became commonplace, eggs were
replaced by mayonnaise-based concoctions
to ensure food safety.

½ cup (115 g) mayonnaise
½ cup (120 ml) extra-virgin olive oil
1 clove garlic, crushed
2 tablespoons (28 ml) lemon juice
1 tablespoon (15 ml) cider vinegar
2 tablespoons (28 ml) vermouth
1 teaspoon Worcestershire sauce
2 tablespoons (18 g) capers, drained and crushed
½ teaspoon anchovy paste (optional)
⅓ cup (35 g) finely grated Parmesan cheese
⅔ cup (53 g) shredded Parmesan cheese
8 cups (440 g) sliced romaine lettuce

ENGLISH MUFFIN CROUTONS:
1 English muffin
Butter and Parmesan cheese

Combine mayonnaise, olive oil, garlic, lemon juice, vinegar,
vermouth, Worcestershire sauce, capers, and anchovy paste in a
bowl or 1-quart (1-L) glass measuring cup and blend with a wire
whisk. Blend in the ⅓ cup (35 g) of finely grated Parmesan cheese.
In a large salad bowl, toss dressing with romaine, shredded
Parmesan cheese, and croutons.

For English muffin croutons: Split an English muffin in half and
lightly toast. Butter while warm and sprinkle with grated Parmesan
cheese. Run under broiler to lightly brown cheese. Cut into cubes
and allow to cool to room temperature.

Prep = 10 minutes   **Cook** = 5 to 8 minutes
Yield = 4 to 6 servings

Orange Blossom Salad with Champagne Dressing

This recipe harkens from a tearoom of decades ago that served a wonderful luncheon salad of romaine lettuce tossed with creamy, orange-flavored Champagne dressing. For the sake of convenience, foil-wrapped candied walnuts can be used, although the end result is somewhat sweeter.

1½	cups (340 g)	mayonnaise
½	cup (120 ml)	Champagne
¼	cup (70 g)	frozen orange juice concentrate, thawed
8 to 10	cups (440 to 550 g)	sliced romaine lettuce
1	cup (160 g)	red or green seedless grapes, halved
1	cup (190 g)	canned mandarin orange segments, drained
1 ½	cups (225 g)	julienne strips of baked ham
1	cup (120 g)	toasted or candied walnuts*

In a bowl or 1-quart (1-L) glass measuring cup, blend together mayonnaise, Champagne, and orange juice concentrate with a wire whisk. Combine lettuce, grapes, orange segments, ham, and half the walnuts in a large salad bowl. Add enough dressing to moisten ingredients and toss. (It's a personal preference as to how much dressing to use.) Serve salad on individual plates and garnish with remaining walnuts.

*To toast walnuts: Preheat oven to 350°F (180°C, or gas mark 4) and spread walnuts on a baking sheet. Toast for 6 to 8 minutes, turning once, until golden brown. Watch carefully to avoid burning.

Prep = 15 minutes **Cook** = 6 to 8 minutes
Yield = 6 to 8 servings

Celery Root Remoulade

In Europe, celeriac, or celery knobs, are often served
as coleslaw or a garnish on cold plates. A Swiss-inspired
inn in the Litchfield Hills area of Connecticut used to serve
celery root remoulade with Bündnerteller, an air-dried
beef appetizer. This version is unique in that the
celery root is blanched in Riesling wine.

- 2 medium celery roots
- 2 cups (480 ml) Riesling wine
- 1 tablespoon (15 g) Düsseldorf or Dijon mustard
- 1 tablespoon (15 ml) lemon juice
- 1 cup (225 g) mayonnaise
- Salt and pepper

Pare celery roots. Cut into slices about 1/16 inch (2 mm) thick and
then cut slices into matchstick strips. Put celery root in a large
mixing bowl. Bring wine to a boil and pour over celery root. Cover
with plastic wrap and refrigerate for at least 2 hours. Meanwhile,
combine mustard, lemon juice, and mayonnaise. Remove celery
root from the refrigerator and pour off wine. Toss with mayonnaise mixture and season with salt and pepper to taste.

Prep = 15 minutes   **Cook** = 5 minutes   **Yield** = 4 to 6 servings

Dilled Cucumbers
in Chablis

Cucumbers with dill are one of the
lightest salads that can be served. Even if sour cream is
added, it has much less fat than oil or mayonnaise would
add. Traditionally, this recipe calls for vinegar and
water. Chablis or any white wine will give it a
distinctive flavor.

- 1 large English cucumber
- ⅓ cup (80 ml) white vinegar
- ⅓ cup (80 ml) Chablis
- 2 tablespoons (26 g) sugar
- ½ teaspoon salt
- ⅛ teaspoon pepper
- 1 tablespoon (4 g) minced fresh dill
- ⅔ cup (155 g) sour cream (optional)

Peel and thinly slice cucumber. Combine cucumber with vinegar, Chablis, sugar, salt, and pepper in a covered container. Refrigerate for 3 to 8 hours to blend flavors. Drain cucumbers, sprinkle with dill, and return to refrigerator until ready to serve. At this stage, you may stir in sour cream.

Prep = 10 minutes **Cook** = 3 to 8 hours **Yield** = 4 servings

Salade Niçoise

For years restaurants served Salade Niçoise with fully cooked (usually canned) tuna. Now, many serve it with a seared fillet of tuna instead.

8 ounces (225 g) tuna fillet
  ½ cup (120 ml) Sauvignon Blanc or other white wine
  ½ teaspoon Worcestershire sauce
  1 tablespoon (15 ml) olive oil
    Salt and pepper
  1 large head Bibb or Boston lettuce, torn into bite-size pieces
  1 pound (455 g) French green beans, cooked and chilled
  2 medium-size ripe tomatoes, sliced into wedges
  2 hard-cooked eggs, peeled and quartered
  ¼ cup (25 g) sliced ripe olives
  6 anchovy fillets (optional)

FRENCH DRESSING:
  1 cup (240 ml) extra-virgin olive oil
  1 clove garlic, crushed
  ¼ cup (60 ml) cider vinegar
  2 tablespoons (28 ml) fresh lemon juice
  ¼ cup (60 ml) Sauvignon Blanc or other white wine
  1 tablespoon (15 g) Dijon mustard
  ½ teaspoon Worcestershire sauce
  ½ teaspoon salt
  ½ teaspoon cracked black pepper

Place tuna in a shallow bowl and cover with a mixture of wine and Worcestershire sauce. Cover with plastic and marinate in the refrigerator for 1 hour. Remove tuna from wine. Pat dry with towel and rub with olive oil. Sprinkle with salt and pepper. Place a medium skillet over medium-high heat. Sear tuna on both sides for about 2 minutes on each side. Remove from heat and slice.

For French Dressing: Combine olive oil, garlic, vinegar, lemon juice, wine, mustard, Worcestershire sauce, salt, and pepper in a 1-quart (1-L) glass measuring cup or mixing bowl. Blend with wire whisk. Chill in refrigerator at least 2 hours.

Arrange lettuce in a deep platter or salad bowl and arrange beans, tomatoes, and eggs around the edge of the lettuce. Mound sliced, seared tuna in the center and garnish with olives and anchovy fillets. Drizzle some dressing over the salad and serve the remainder on the side.

Prep = 20 minutes **Cook** = 5 minutes **Yield** = 6 servings

Tuscan White Bean Salad with White Wine

Cannellini beans simmered in Pinot Grigio
grace this classic Italian salad with a Tuscan accent.
The secret to cooking tender beans lies in soaking
them for at least 3 to 4 hours beforehand.

- ½   pound (225 g) dried cannellini beans
- 1   quart (945 ml) water
- 2   cups (480 ml) Pinot Grigio or white wine
- 2   cups (480 ml) water
- 1   whole onion, quartered
- ½   teaspoon salt
- 1   bay leaf
- ¼   cup (60 ml) olive oil
- 6   tablespoons (90 ml) cooking liquid from beans
- ½   cup (120 ml) lemon juice
- ½   teaspoon salt
- ½   teaspoon pepper
- 1   pint (300 g) grape tomatoes, quartered
- ⅓   cup (30 g) chopped parsley
- ½   cup (50 g) sliced scallions
- 2   tablespoons (8 g) chopped fresh basil leaves
-     Romaine lettuce leaves

In a large saucepan, soak beans in 1 quart (945 ml) of water for 3
to 4 hours, then drain. Add 2 cups (480 ml) each of wine and
water, onion, salt, and bay leaf. Bring to a boil, reduce heat to low,
cover, and simmer until beans are tender, approximately 1 hour.

Cool beans. Combine olive oil, reserved liquid from beans,
lemon juice, salt, and pepper in a glass measuring cup and toss
over beans. Add tomatoes, parsley, scallions, and basil. Cover
and chill for at least 2 hours. Serve in a bowl lined with romaine
lettuce leaves.

Prep = 20 minutes   **Cook** = 1 hour   **Chill** = 2 hours
Yield = 12 servings

Warm Dandelion Greens Salad

This is a change of pace from the traditional hot spinach salad. Baby dandelion greens are much more delicate than their adult counterpart and are rich with health benefits. The secret to serving these or any greens with a warm dressing is not to overtoss them and to serve it immediately. The salad should never completely wilt.

8   slices bacon
¼   cup (40 g) minced shallots
1   tablespoon (13 g) sugar
¼   teaspoon dry mustard
3   tablespoons (45 ml) red wine vinegar
3   tablespoons (45 ml) red wine
1   teaspoon dried mixed salad herbs
10 cups (300 g) baby dandelion greens, washed and dried

Sauté bacon in medium skillet until crisp, then set aside and crumble, reserving bacon grease. Add shallots to bacon grease in skillet. Sauté until transparent. Add sugar, mustard, vinegar, red wine, and salad herbs. Heat through and toss with dandelion greens and crumbled bacon.

Prep = 10 minutes   **Cook** = 12 minutes
Yield = 6 servings

Overnight Salad

It is nearly a cultural mandate that a version of this salad must appear in every Junior League cookbook across the United States. In this recipe, hearts of palm and white wine are added. To prevent the lettuce from browning, always cut it with a plastic knife.

- 1 large head iceberg lettuce
- ½ cup (50 g) sliced scallions
- 1 can (8 ounces, or 225 g) water chestnuts, drained and sliced
- 1 cup (145 g) sliced, drained hearts of palm
- 1 cup (130 g) frozen peas, thawed
- 2 cups (450 g) mayonnaise
- 2 tablespoons (28 ml) white wine
- 2 teaspoons (8 g) sugar
- ¼ teaspoon garlic powder
- 1 teaspoon seasoned salt
- ½ pound (225 g) bacon, cooked crisp and crumbled
- 1 large tomato, seeded and chopped
- 4 hard-cooked eggs, chilled and chopped

Cut lettuce into small pieces and line a 9 × 13-inch (22.5 × 32.5-cm) casserole dish. Cover with scallions, water chestnuts, hearts of palm, and peas. In a small bowl, blend mayonnaise, white wine, sugar, garlic powder, and salt. Spread over salad mixture. Cover with plastic wrap and refrigerate overnight. Just before serving, sprinkle with bacon, tomato, and egg.

Prep = 15 minutes   **Cook** = 8 hours   **Yield** = 8 servings

Hearts of Romaine with Garlic Wine Dressing

Hearts of romaine are the paler green inner leaves that have a slightly sweeter taste than the dark outer ones. This recipe creates a nice alternative to Caesar dressing, for a simple green salad.

3   medium heads romaine lettuce
6   tablespoons (90 ml) olive oil
2   tablespoons (28 g) mayonnaise
2   tablespoons (28 ml) white wine vinegar
2   tablespoons (28 ml) dry white wine
2   cloves garlic, crushed
1   tablespoon (4 g) minced chives
    Salt and pepper

Remove dark outer leaves from romaine heads and reserve for another use. Split heads in half, lengthwise. Gently wash any soil that might be in the center while keeping them intact. Pat dry with paper towels.

In a small bowl, whisk olive oil, mayonnaise, white wine vinegar, white wine, crushed garlic, and chives. Season with salt and pepper to taste. Arrange each slice of romaine lettuce, cut side up, on individual salad plates and drizzle with dressing.

Prep = 15 minutes   **Cook** = N/A   **Yield** = 6 servings

Sautéed Chicken Salad with Sherry

This recipe was inspired by a hot chicken salad once served at Maxwell's Plum in New York City. During its heyday, the Back Room became a favorite lunch hangout after taping cooking spots on *Midday Live* at WNEW.

    4   boneless, skinless chicken breast halves
        Salt and pepper
    ¼   cup (60 ml) olive oil
    1   clove garlic, crushed
    ¼   cup (40 g) minced shallots
    2   tablespoons (28 ml) tarragon vinegar
    1   teaspoon (5 g) Dijon mustard
    ½   cup (120 ml) sherry
    8   cups (240 g) mesclun mix

Cut chicken breast into strips and sprinkle lightly with salt and pepper. Pour olive oil into a large skillet and add garlic, shallots, and chicken. Sauté until chicken is golden and tender, 8 to 10 minutes. Wisk vinegar and mustard together until blended. Stir in sherry and add to pan, heat through, stirring to deglaze browned bits. Divide mesclun among four plates and spoon chicken and sauce over greens.

Prep = 10 minutes   **Cook** = 10 to 14 minutes   **Yield** = 4 servings

Strawberry-Merlot Citrus Salad

The recipe makes a generous serving of dressing, so there are plenty of leftovers. This sweet, fruity dressing complements any combination of greens and pairs especially well with chicken.

1	cup (240 ml) extra-virgin olive oil
½	cup (120 ml) hazelnut oil
½	cup (120 ml) Merlot
½	cup(142 g) frozen orange juice concentrate
3	tablespoons (45 ml) fresh lemon juice
1 ½	teaspoons grated orange peel
2	cloves garlic, crushed
1	tablespoon (4 g) fresh minced thyme
2	bags (10 ounces, or 280 g, each) baby spinach
2	navel oranges, peeled and sectioned
1	pint (290 g) strawberries, hulled and halved
⅔	cup (90 g) toasted hazelnuts*

Combine olive oil, hazelnut oil, Merlot, orange juice concentrate, lemon juice, orange peel, garlic, and thyme in a bowl and blend with a wire whisk. Pour in jar and chill in the refrigerator. Combine baby spinach, oranges, and strawberries and ⅓ cup (45 g) of hazelnuts in a large salad bowl. Toss with enough dressing to moisten leaves; serve on individual plates, garnished with remaining hazelnuts.*

*To toast hazelnuts: Preheat oven to 350°F (180°C, or gas mark 4) and spread hazelnuts on a baking sheet. Toast for 6 to 8 minutes, stirring once, until golden brown. Watch carefully to avoid burning.

Prep = 10 minutes **Cook** = 6 to 8 minutes **Yield** = 6 servings

Tabbouleh

This new spin on the traditional Middle Eastern
salad, filled with tomatoes, green onions, and cucumber,
features bulgur that has soaked in wine.

¾ cup (150 g) uncooked bulgur
White wine
1 ½ cups (90 g) minced fresh parsley
2 cups (360 g) seeded tomatoes, coarsely chopped
1 cup (35 g) seeded cucumber, coarsely chopped
½ cup (50 g) sliced scallions
2 tablespoons (12 g) chopped fresh mint
⅓ cup (80 ml) extra-virgin olive oil
⅓ cup (870 ml) fresh lemon juice
Salt and pepper

In a small bowl, cover bulgur with as much wine as is needed.
Let stand for 30 minutes and drain, pressing out as much liquid as
possible. Place bulgur, parsley, tomatoes, cucumber, scallions, and
mint in a bowl. Wisk olive oil, lemon juice, and salt and pepper
until blended. Toss with bulgur mixture. Cover and chill at least
2 hours to blend flavors.

Prep = 35 minutes **Chill** = 2 hours **Yield** = 6 servings

The Great European
Classics

Beef Bourguignon

Cooking with wine evokes images of French bistros, crusty baguettes, and Beef Bourguignon. This version of the iconic stew, however, does not include potatoes as they tend to break down in the sauce. Simple garlic-roasted new potatoes served with the stew are equally evocative.

8 slices bacon, cut into 1-inch (2.5-cm) squares
2 pounds (905 g) chuck or round roast, cut into 1-inch (2.5-cm) cubes
2 cups (480 ml) dry red wine (preferably Burgundy)
2 teaspoons beef bouillon granules
1 clove garlic, crushed
1 whole onion, sliced in half
   bouquet garni*
4 tablespoons (55 g) butter
8 ounces (225 g) button mushrooms, halved
1 bag (16 ounces, or 455 g) frozen pearl onions, thawed
¼ cup (31 g) all-purpose flour

Cook bacon in a large stockpot or Dutch oven until crisp and set aside. Brown meat in bacon drippings. Add wine, bouillon granules, garlic, onion, and bouquet garni. Bring to a boil, cover, and simmer for 1½ hours, or until meat is tender. Remove bouquet garni. Melt butter in a large skillet and sauté mushrooms and pearl onions until tender. Blend in flour and transfer the mushrooms and pearl onions into the Beef Bourguignon. Add bacon. Blend together and continue cooking for about 10 minutes, or until sauce has thickened.

*To make bouquet garni: Combine 2 bay leaves, 4 parsley sprigs, 1 teaspoon (1.4 g) dried thyme, and 1 teaspoon (0.6 g) dried marjoram in a cheesecloth and tie with a string.

Prep = 20 minutes   **Cook** = 1¾ hours   **Yield** = 6 servings

Beef Filet Stroganoff

Once considered exotic, beef stroganoff was the fare of fine restaurants in the 1960s—at about the same time that *Dr. Zhivago* was the "it" movie at the Oscars.

1 ½ pounds (680 g) beef tenderloin
2 tablespoons (28 g) butter
1 clove garlic, crushed
8 ounces (225 g) sliced mushrooms
1 cup (240 ml) beef broth
½ cup (120 ml) dry red wine
2 tablespoons (30 g) ketchup
1 teaspoon Worcestershire sauce
1 teaspoon salt
½ cup (50 g) sliced scallions
¼ cup (32 g) all-purpose flour
1 cup (230 g) sour cream
4 cups (640 g) cooked egg noodles, rice, or couscous

Slice beef across grain into 1 × 1½-inch (2.5 × 3.75-cm) strips. In a large skillet, melt butter over medium heat. Stir-fry beef in butter until browned. Add garlic and mushrooms and continue cooking for about 3 minutes. Reserve ⅓ cup (80 ml) beef broth for thickening. Combine remaining broth, red wine, ketchup, Worcestershire sauce, salt, and scallions. Pour over beef and mushrooms. Cover and simmer for 10 minutes, or until beef is tender.

Blend reserved ⅓ cup (80 ml) broth and flour until mixed into a very smooth paste with no lumps. Gradually blend into beef mixture, stirring constantly. Boil, stirring for 1 minute, reduce heat to low. Blend in sour cream and heat through, but do not boil or sour cream may curdle. Serve hot over noodles, couscous, or rice.

Prep = 15 minutes   **Cook** = 15 to 18 minutes   **Yield** = 6 servings

Chicken Cacciatore

Cacciatore means "hunter" in Italian. Traditional "hunter style" treatment is also seen with rabbit. It is similar to Chicken Marengo, a dish thought to have been served to Napoleon Bonaparte after the battle of Marengo in 1800. He considered it his lucky dish.

½ cup (63 g) all-purpose flour
½ teaspoon salt
1 whole chicken (about 3½ pounds, or 1.6 kg), cut up
¼ cup (60 ml) olive oil
1 medium green bell pepper, seeded and chopped
1 medium red bell pepper, seeded and chopped
½ cup (80 g) minced shallots
1 cup (70 g) sliced mushrooms
1 can (14.5 ounces, or 411 g) diced tomatoes, drained
1 can (8 ounce, or 225 g) tomato sauce
1 cup (240 ml) dry white wine
½ cup (50 g) sliced ripe olives
  Parmesan cheese

Combine flour with salt in a shallow dish and dredge chicken in flour. Heat olive oil in a large skillet and brown chicken on all sides until even in color (about 15 minutes). Add bell peppers, shallots, mushrooms, tomatoes, tomato sauce, wine, and olives. Cover and simmer for 30 to 40 minutes, or until chicken is tender. Serve with Parmesan cheese at the table.

Prep = 15 minutes **Cook** = 45 to 55 minutes **Yield** = 6 servings

Canard à l'Orange

Fact: Ducks shrink. Anyone who's ever tried
to feed eight friends a classic French dinner of
Canard à l'orange from one 5-pound (2.3-kg) duck has
discovered this, too. A roasted duck will end up a fraction of
the size it appears when frozen. The technique presented
here is "restaurant style," where each serving is a
semi-boneless half. Not basting with sauce while
roasting will result in a very crisp skin.

2   (3½-pound, or 1.6-kg) ducklings, thawed if frozen
    Salt
1   cup (200 g) sugar
1   tablespoon (15 ml) lemon juice
¼   cup (60 ml) red wine vinegar
¼   cup (60 ml) red wine
1   tablespoon (8 g) cornstarch mixed with 1 tablespoon (15 ml) water
1½ cups (355 ml) orange juice
    Julienned zest of 1 orange
1   tablespoon (15 ml) orange liqueur
½   cup (160 g) currant jelly
1   tablespoon (14 g) butter
    Wild rice or mashed sweet potatoes

Prep = 20 minutes   **Cook** = 2¼ to 2¾ hours   **Yield** = 4 servings

Preheat oven to 350°F (180°C, or gas mark 4). Remove neck and giblets from cavities of ducks. Fold wing tips under wings and fasten the neck skin to duckling with back of skewer. Pierce skin of ducks all over and lightly sprinkle with salt. Place ducks breast-side up, in a roasting pan. Roast, uncovered for about 2 to 2½ hours, until crisp.

Meanwhile, prepare sauce: In a large, heavy-bottomed saucepan, over medium heat, heat sugar and lemon juice, stirring constantly, until it's a rich, amber brown. Remove from heat and add vinegar and wine to deglaze pan (stand back because it will foam up). Combine cornstarch mixture with orange juice, orange zest, and orange liqueur. Return to heat, stirring constantly until mixture thickens and boils. Remove from heat and blend in currant jelly and butter until both have melted.

Split ducks in half and remove rib bones, leaving leg and wing bones intact. Place duck halves, skin-side up, on roasting-pan rack. Return to oven for 8 to 15 minutes longer to recrisp skin. Spoon sauce over duck halves on plates. Serve with wild rice or mashed sweet potatoes.

Chateaubriand with Sauce Bordelaise

Duchess potatoes piped through a pastry
bag and bouquets of mixed vegetables traditionally
surround this dish fit for kings.

1   beef tenderloin (2½ to 3 pounds, 1.1 to 1.4 kg)
1   tablespoon (14 g) softened butter or olive oil
2   cloves garlic, crushed
½   teaspoon dried marjoram leaves
¼   teaspoon coarse kosher salt or sea salt
¼   teaspoon cracked pepper
⅓   cup (80 ml) red wine

SAUCE BORDELAISE:
4   tablespoons (55 g) butter
½   cup (80 g) minced shallots
1   clove garlic, crushed
¼   cup (32 g) all-purpose flour
1   can (10½ ounces, or 315 ml) condensed beef broth
½   cup (120 ml) dry red wine
1   tablespoon (4 g) minced fresh parsley
¼   teaspoon dried thyme
1   bay leaf
¼   teaspoon salt
½   teaspoon Worcestershire sauce

Assorted vegetables and mashed or roasted new potatoes

Prep = 25 minutes   **Cook** = 35 to 50 minutes   **Yield** = 6 servings

Preheat oven to 425°F (220°C, or gas mark 7). Tuck small end or "tail" of tenderloin back under beef by about 6 inches (15 cm) and tie in place with string at about 1½-inch (3.75-cm) intervals. Slather tenderloin with butter and coat surface with garlic, marjoram, salt, and pepper. Place in shallow roasting pan and insert a meat thermometer in the thickest part of the tenderloin. For medium rare: roast for 35 to 40 minutes, or until thermometer reads 135°F (57°C). Remove from oven and let meat rest with a tent of aluminum foil over it for 15 minutes. This allows the temperature to rise another 10 degrees, making meat easier to carve. For medium: roast, uncovered, for 45 to 50 minutes, or until thermometer reads 150°F (66°C). Allow meat to rest for 15 minutes under a foil tent until the thermometer reaches 160°F (71°C). Cut string from roast and transfer meat to serving platter. Heat wine in bottom of roasting pan to deglaze, and mix with drippings and add to Sauce Bordelaise. Serve Chateaubriand on a platter surrounded by vegetables and potatoes.

For Sauce Bordelaise: Melt butter in a medium saucepan and sauté shallots and garlic until shallots are transparent. Blend in flour and continue to cook, stirring constantly, until flour is a rich, golden brown. Blend in beef broth, wine, parsley, thyme, bay leaf, salt, and Worcestershire sauce. Continue cooking and stirring until sauce comes to a boil and is thickened. Discard bay leaf.

Coquilles Saint Jacques

Coquilles Saint Jacques is a mainstay in traditional, haute cuisine French restaurants. Times change and menus evolve, but this dish still appears in bistros serving French comfort food.

1 pound (455 g) sea scallops

1 ¼ cups (295 ml) dry white wine such as Sauvignon Blanc

1 cup (240 ml) water

½ small onion, sliced

1 bay leaf

½ teaspoon salt

¼ teaspoon pepper

¾ stick (83 g, or 6 tablespoons) unsalted butter, divided

½ pound (225 g) small mushrooms

1 egg yolk

½ cup (120 ml) heavy cream

1 tablespoon (8 g) all-purpose flour

½ cup (25 g) fresh bread crumbs, lightly toasted

½ cup (50 g) grated Parmesan cheese

1 tablespoon (4 g) minced fresh parsley

Remove tough muscle from the side of each scallop and cut into ¾-inch (1.9-cm) pieces. Bring wine, water, onion, bay leaf, salt, and pepper to a boil in a large saucepan. Boil for 5 minutes. Add scallops and simmer for just about 3 minutes, until scallops are no longer transparent.

Remove scallops with a slotted spoon and transfer to a plate. Return any onions back to the liquid and return to a boil until reduced to 1 cup (240 ml), 8 to 10 minutes. Strain liquid into a large measuring cup.

Melt 2 tablespoons (28 g) butter in a large skillet and sauté mushrooms until most of the moisture has evaporated. Set mushrooms aside while preparing sauce. Whisk egg yolk with heavy cream in a small bowl. Melt another 2 tablespoons (28 g) butter in a medium saucepan. Whisk in flour until blended, making a roux. Gradually add cooking liquid while whisking, and continue whisking and cooking until thickened. Blend a little of the hot liquid into the egg-yolk mixture, then blend back into the sauce and heat through. Remove from heat and add mushrooms and scallops to the sauce.

Melt remaining 2 tablespoons (28 g) butter in a saucepan. Remove from heat and stir in bread crumbs, Parmesan cheese, and parsley. Divide scallop mixture into scallop shells or ramekins and top with bread crumbs. Broil about 2 inches (5 cm) from heat, until golden.

Prep = 20 minutes **Cook** = 35 minutes **Yield** = 8 servings

Coq au Vin Blanc

Isn't coq au vin the quintessential dish calling
for cooking with wine? Coq au vin is usually cooked
in red wine, but this version featuring
Chardonnay is masterful.

½ cup (63 g) all-purpose flour
1 teaspoon salt
¼ teaspoon pepper
1 chicken (3½ pounds, or 1.6 kg), cut up
4 strips bacon
8 ounces (225 g) sliced cremini mushrooms
1 package (10 ounces, or 280 g) frozen pearl onions
2 medium carrots, sliced
2 medium parsnips, sliced
1 clove garlic, crushed
1½ cups (355 ml) chicken broth
2 cups (480 ml) Chardonnay
2 large celery stalks, sliced
   bouquet garni*

In a small dish, mix flour with salt and pepper. Dredge chicken in
flour. In a large skillet over medium heat, fry bacon until crisp and
remove with a slotted spoon to drain on paper towels. Brown
chicken in bacon fat, turning on all sides (about 15 minutes) until
even in color. Remove chicken and add mushrooms and onions,
stirring until mushrooms are tender.

Drain all fat from skillet. Add chicken back to mushrooms, along
with carrots parsnips, garlic, chicken broth, and Chardonnay.

Add celery stalks and bouquet garni. Cover and simmer about
40 to 45 minutes, or until chicken is tender.

*To make bouquet garni: Combine 2 bay leaves, 4 parsley sprigs,
1 teaspoon (1.4 g) dried thyme, and 1 teaspoon (0.6 g) dried
marjoram in a cheesecloth and tie with a string.

Prep = 15 minutes **Cook** = 1 hour and 20 to 30 minutes
Yield = 6 servings

Choucroute Garnie

Choucroute is a hallmark of Alsatian cuisine.
It is essentially a wine-braised, sauerkraut-based
casserole topped with copious quantities of pork-based
meats and sausages. There are many variations,
but all require a hearty appetite.

2   bags (16 ounces, or 455 g, each) sauerkraut
½   pound (225 g) thick-sliced bacon
½   cup (80 g) chopped shallots
1   bag (10 ounces, or 280 g) frozen pearl onions, thawed
2   carrots, peeled and sliced
1   yellow turnip, peeled and sliced
2   tart, firm apples, cored and chopped (do not peel)
6   smoked pork chops
2   cups (480 ml) Riesling or white wine
2   cups (480 ml) chicken broth
6   bratwurst
6   knackwurst
2   teaspoons caraway seeds
    bouquet garni*

Soak sauerkraut in water for half an hour and rinse well. Slice
bacon into squares and cook in a large skillet. When most of the
fat has been rendered off, add shallots, onions, carrots, and turnip.
Cook, stirring occasionally, until vegetables have started to
caramelize. Add apples and continue cooking for 5 minutes longer.
    Preheat oven to 350°F (180°C, or gas mark 4). Drain sauer-
kraut and squeeze out all of the water. Spread into the bottom of
a large casserole and top with pork chops. Cover pork chops with
vegetable mixture. Sprinkle with caraway seeds and tuck bouquet
garni in center of casserole. Pour wine and chicken broth over
pork chops. Place a buttered sheet of baking parchment against
pork chops and bake for 1½ to 2 hours, or until most of the liquid
has evaporated but the chops are not dry. During the last half
hour of baking, grill knackwurst and bratwurst until skins start to
pop. Remove parchment, arrange sausages on top of casserole,
and serve.

*To make bouquet garni: Combine 2 bay leaves, 4 parsley sprigs,
10 juniper berries, and 6 peppercorns in a cheesecloth and tie
with a string.

Prep = 30 minutes   **Cook** = 1½ to 2 hours   **Yield** = 6 servings

Osso Buco
alla Milanese

This classic dish of braised veal shanks with
aromatic gremolata, an herb sauce featuring citrus peel
and white wine, hails from Milan. Traditionally, osso buco
was made without tomatoes, as they were unknown in
Milan until the late nineteenth century. For authentic
side dishes, pair osso buco with polenta, risotto,
or mashed potatoes.

6   veal shanks, cross cut 2½ inches (6.25 cm) thick
½   teaspoon salt
¼   teaspoon pepper
¼   cup (32 g) all-purpose flour
2   tablespoons (30 ml) extra-virgin olive oil
⅔   cup (160 ml) dry white wine
1   can (10.5 ounces, or 315 ml) beef broth
1   can (16 ounces, or 455 g) stewed tomatoes
1   clove garlic, crushed
1   bay leaf
2   teaspoons grated lemon peel
2   tablespoons (8 g) chopped fresh parsley

Sprinkle veal with salt and pepper and coat with flour. In a large
(4-quart, or 3.8-L) stockpot with lid, brown veal shanks in olive oil
on both sides. Add wine, beef broth, garlic, bay leaf, and 1 teaspoon lemon peel. Heat to boiling. Cover and reduce heat; simmer
for 1½ to 2 hours. Remove veal and place on serving platter; keep
warm. Skim fat from broth and remove bay leaf. Boil down broth
until somewhat syrupy and spoon over veal shanks. Sprinkle with
remaining lemon peel and parsley to garnish.

Prep = 15 minutes   **Cook** = 2 to 2¼ hours   **Yield** = 6 servings

Contemporary Cassoulet

Cassoulet is a legendary specialty of Languedoc,
the southwestern region of France that includes Toulouse,
Castlenaudary, and Carcassone. Early attempts at re-creating
this authentic signature dish were thwarted by ingredients
like *confit d'oie*, or preserved goose. The process seemed
to take days of preparation. This version is a little
more efficient.

8   chicken thighs
    Salt and pepper
3   cloves garlic, crushed
2   parsnips, peeled and sliced
1   large onion, chopped
1   large red bell pepper, seeded and chopped
2   cans (15 ounces, or 420 g, each) cannellini beans, drained
1   can (14 ounces, or 400 g) Italian-style stewed tomatoes
1   cup (240 ml) chicken broth
1   cup (240 ml) white wine
1   tablespoon (4 g) minced fresh parsley
1   teaspoon dried thyme
2   bay leaves
8   ounces (225 g) kielbasa or garlic sausage,
    sliced into ½-inch (1.25-cm) rounds
1   cup (50 g) fresh bread crumbs

Prep = 30 minutes   **Cook** = 1¾ to 2 hours   **Yield** = 6 to 8 servings

Preheat oven to 400°F (200°C, or gas mark 6). Place chicken thighs in a 9 × 13-inch (22.5 × 32.5-cm) roasting pan and sprinkle with salt and pepper. Bake for 40 to 45 minutes, or until skin is very crispy. Save rendered fat (at least ¼ cup [60 ml]). Remove bones but not skin from chicken. Cut thighs into quarters. Pour 2 tablespoons (28 ml) reserved chicken fat into a medium skillet. Sauté garlic, parsnips, onion, and bell pepper in pan until tender. Combine beans, tomatoes, chicken broth, wine, parsley, thyme, and bay leaves in a slow cooker.

Wash out skillet and sauté sausage until golden brown. Add sausage to slow cooker, along with chicken. Cover and cook on low for 7 to 8 hours. Remove bay leaves and spoon mixture into a 4-quart (3.8-L) casserole dish. Melt 2 tablespoons (28 g) reserved chicken fat in skillet and toss around bread crumbs, coating them well. Cover casserole with crumbs. Preheat oven to 350°F (180°C, or gas mark 4) and bake casserole for 30 to 45 minutes, or until topping has browned.

Sherried Shepherd's Pie

Shepherd's pie is classic pub fare on both sides of the Atlantic, and no two establishments' recipes are exactly alike. This favorite rendition contains sherry for a dose of zing for this comfort food.

2   pounds (905 g) potatoes, such as russet, peeled and cubed
2   tablespoons (30 g) sour cream
1   large egg yolk
½   cup (120 ml) cream (for a lighter version, substitute vegetable or chicken broth)
    Salt and freshly ground black pepper
1   tablespoon (15 ml) extra-virgin olive oil
1¾ pounds (785 g) ground beef or ground lamb
1   carrot, peeled and chopped
1   onion, chopped
3   tablespoons (42 g) butter
3   tablespoons (24 g) all-purpose flour
1   cup (240 ml) beef stock or broth
½   cup (120 ml) sherry
2   teaspoons (10 ml) Worcestershire sauce
¾   cup (98 g) frozen peas
1   teaspoon sweet paprika
2   tablespoons (8 g) chopped fresh parsley leaves

Boil potatoes in salted water until tender, about 12 minutes. Drain potatoes and pour them into a bowl. Combine sour cream, egg yolk, and cream. Add the cream mixture to potatoes and mash until potatoes are almost smooth. Season to taste with salt and pepper.

Preheat a large skillet over medium-high heat. Pour oil into hot pan, add meat. Season meat with salt and pepper. Brown and crumble meat for 3 or 4 minutes. If you are using lamb and the pan is fatty, spoon away some of the drippings. Add chopped carrot and onion to the meat. Sauté with meat for 5 minutes, stirring frequently. In a small saucepan over medium heat, cook butter and flour together for 2 minutes. Whisk in broth, sherry, and Worcestershire sauce. Thicken gravy for 1 minute. Add gravy to meat and vegetables. Stir in peas. Preheat broiler to high. Fill a small rectangular casserole with the pie filling. Spoon potatoes over meat evenly. Top potatoes with paprika and broil 6 to 8 inches from the heat, until potatoes are evenly browned. Top casserole dish with chopped parsley and serve.

Prep = 20 minutes   **Cook** = 30 to 40 minutes   **Yield** = 8 servings

Chicken Piccata

There are many subtle variations of chicken
piccata—some have an egg-and-cheese batter,
some include capers, and others feature sautéed strips
of ham and mushrooms. What almost all of them
have in common is lemon and white wine.

  2   tablespoons (28 g) butter
1 ½   cups (105 g) sliced mushrooms
  4   ounces (115 g) prosciutto, cut into julienne strips
       (other ham may be substituted)
  ¾   cup (94 g) all-purpose flour
  1   teaspoon salt
  6   boneless, skinless chicken breast halves
  6   tablespoons (90 ml) olive oil
  ¾   cup (175 ml) freshly squeezed lemon juice
  1   cup (240 ml) white wine
  ½   cup (35 g) minced fresh parsley

In a medium skillet, melt butter and sauté mushrooms and ham
until mushrooms are golden brown and moisture has cooked off.
Set aside while cooking chicken.

Combine flour and salt in a small dish. Dredge chicken in flour.
Heat olive oil in a large skillet and sauté chicken until golden on
both sides. Add lemon juice, wine, and parsley. Continue cooking
for 5 or 6 minutes, or until liquid is reduced by half. Transfer
chicken to serving plates and spoon sauce over the top. Garnish
with ham and mushroom topping.

Prep = 20 minutes   **Cook** = 15 to 20 minutes   **Yield** = 6 servings

Veal Marsala

In a break from the tradition of using button
mushrooms in Veal Marsala, try a few cremini mushrooms
instead. If cremini mushrooms are unavailable, chopped
portobello mushrooms also work well.
Meatier mushrooms gives this classic
dish even more character.

  4   veal scallops, about 6 ounces (170 g) each
 ½   cup (63 g) all-purpose flour
 ¼   teaspoon salt
 ¼   teaspoon pepper
  3   tablespoons (45 ml) extra-virgin olive oil
  2   cloves garlic, crushed
  1   cup (70 g) sliced cremini mushrooms or chopped portobello
       mushrooms
 ¼   cup (16 g) minced fresh parsley
 ¾   cup (175 ml) dry Marsala wine
       Pasta or polenta

Pound veal scallops between plastic wrap until they are about ¼
inch (6 mm) thick. Combine four, salt and pepper in a pie plate or
shallow dish. Dredge scallops in flour mixture. Heat oil in a large
skillet over medium heat and brown veal on both sides. Set aside
and add mushrooms and garlic to skillet, cooking until mushrooms are tender. Add veal back to the skillet along with parsley
and wine. Simmer for another 8 to 10 minutes. Serve with pasta
or polenta.

Prep = 20 minutes   **Cook** = 30 minutes   **Yield** = 4 servings

Veal Parmigiana Chianti

This version of the all-time favorite incorporates
a sauce simmered with Chianti. If time is in short
supply, replace the homemade Italian Tomato Sauce
with a 16-ounce (455-g) jar of sauce. Add the Chianti to
the jarred sauce and simmer together for about 10 minutes
before baking with the veal. Always serve veal
parmigiana with pasta or polenta.

¼	cup (32 g) all-purpose flour
1	large egg
2	tablespoons (30 ml) water
⅔	cups (77 g) dry bread crumbs
⅓	cup (33 g) grated Parmesan cheese
6	veal scallops
6 to 8	tablespoons (90 to 120 ml) extra-virgin olive oil

ITALIAN TOMATO SAUCE:

2	slices bacon
1	tablespoon (15 ml) olive oil
½	cup (80 g) chopped onion
2	cloves garlic, crushed
½	cup (75 g) chopped and seeded green bell pepper
1	can (14 ounces, or 400 g) whole tomatoes, undrained
1	can (8 ounces, or 225 g) tomato sauce
½	cup (120 ml) Chianti
1	tablespoon (4 g) minced fresh basil, or 1 teaspoon dried
1	tablespoon (4 g) minced fresh oregano, or 1 teaspoon dried
½	teaspoon fennel seeds
2	cups (230 g) shredded mozzarella cheese

Prep = 15 minutes   **Cook** = 45 minutes   **Yield** = 6 servings

Place flour in a small bowl. In another small bowl, beat egg and water. In a third small bowl, combine bread crumbs and Parmesan cheese. Dredge veal scallops in flour, then dip in egg mixture and coat with bread crumbs. In a 12-inch (30-cm) skillet, heat oil over medium heat. Cook 3 scallops of veal at a time for 5 minutes on each side until lightly browned, adding more oil if necessary. Drain veal scallops on paper towels.

Preheat oven to 350°F (180°C, or gas mark 4). Arrange veal scallops in a 7 × 11-inch (17.5 × 27.5-cm) glass baking dish or casserole. Cover with Italian Tomato Sauce and mozzarella cheese. Bake for 25 minutes, until sauce is bubbling and cheese is lightly browned.

For Italian Tomato Sauce: Cut bacon into matchstick pieces and sauté in olive oil until crispy. Add onion, garlic, bell pepper, tomatoes, tomato sauce, Chianti, basil, oregano, and fennel seed. Heat to boiling and simmer, uncovered, for 45 minutes.

Veal Oscar

Veal Oscar is a classic Swedish dish, whose namesake
is King Oscar II of Sweden and Norway. He lived from 1829
to 1907, and historians say this was his favorite dish.

½ cup (63 g) all-purpose flour
1 teaspoon salt
½ teaspoon black pepper
6 veal cutlets, lightly pounded
3 tablespoons (42 g) butter
1 tablespoon (15 ml) olive oil
¼ cup (40 g) minced shallots
¼ cup (60 ml) dry white wine
6 king crab legs, cooked and shelled
2 dozen asparagus spears, cooked tender-crisp

BÉARNAISE SAUCE:
¼ cup (60 ml) dry white wine
¼ cup (60 ml) tarragon vinegar
¼ cup (40 g) minced shallots
1 tablespoon (4 g) minced fresh chives
1 tablespoon (4 g) minced fresh tarragon
3 egg yolks
1 stick (¼ pound, or 112 g) butter, melted

Combine flour, salt, and pepper in a small dish. Dredge cutlets in flour. Melt 2 tablespoons (28 g) butter and 1 tablespoon (15 ml) olive oil in a large nonstick skillet. Sauté cutlets until golden brown (about 3 minutes on each side). Transfer to a warm platter. Melt remaining butter in pan and sauté shallots until tender. Deglaze pan with white wine, adding crabmeat to wine to heat through. Arrange 4 asparagus spears on top of each veal scallop. Top asparagus with crabmeat and spoon Béarnaise Sauce over crab-meat.

For Béarnaise Sauce: In a small saucepan, bring wine, vinegar, shallots, chives, and tarragon to a boil and reduce liquid to half. In a bowl set over a saucepan of simmering water, whisk egg yolks until double in volume. Slowly blend in melted butter until creamy and thickened, and then blend in shallot reduction. Do not allow sauce to overheat or it will curdle and break down.

Prep = 25 minutes   **Cook** = 25 minutes   **Yield** = 6 servings

Slow-Cooker Sauerbraten

There is no need to wait for an Oktoberfest to enjoy sauerbraten with gingersnap gravy. This is a plan-ahead dish, because the longer it is marinated, the better. For side dishes, consider red cabbage and potato pancakes.

1 ¼ cups (295 ml) Riesling wine
1 cup (240 ml) cider vinegar
½ lemon, quartered
2 bay leaves
1 ½ teaspoons salt
½ teaspoon whole peppercorns
½ teaspoon whole cloves
½ teaspoon juniper berries
1 lean top-round roast (4 pounds, or 1.9 kg)
1 tablespoon (14 g) butter
1 tablespoon (8 g) all-purpose flour
¼ cup (60 g) brown sugar
12 gingersnaps, crushed

Combine Riesling wine, vinegar, lemon, bay leaves, salt, pepper-corns, cloves, and juniper berries in a saucepan and bring to a boil. Boil for 2 minutes and let cool. Place roast in a glass casserole dish and pour marinade over meat. Cover with plastic wrap and refrigerate for 24 hours and up to 2 days, turning every 8 hours.

Remove meat and place in slow cooker. Strain marinade and pour over meat. Cook on low for 6 to 7 hours, or until meat starts to fall apart around the edges. Melt butter in a 1-quart (1-L) saucepan and blend in flour, stirring constantly to make a roux. Blend in liquid from slow cooker, along with brown sugar and gingersnaps. Cook, stirring constantly, until gravy is smooth and thickened. Slice sauerbraten on platter and serve with gravy.

Prep = 20 minutes **Chill** = 24 hours **Cook** = 6 to 7 hours
Yield = 6 to 8 servings

Beef, Veal, Pork, and Lamb

Beef Ribs in Molasses-Mustard and Madeira Glaze

In South Carolina, barbecue sauces tend
to be more vinegar- and mustard-based than
tomato-based. This version of beef ribs, inspired by a
dish served at a Southern resort, resulted from
some tinkering with Madeira.

4 ½	pounds beef short ribs
	Salt and pepper
1	cup molasses
⅓	cup (80 ml) cider vinegar
⅓	cup (80 ml) Madeira
⅔	cup Dijon mustard

Preheat oven to 350°F (180°C, or gas mark 4). Place ribs in a 9 ×
13-inch (22.5 × 32.5-cm) pan. Lightly sprinkle with salt and pepper.
Cover and bake for 2 hours. Drain off all of the fat. Combine
molasses, vinegar, Madeira, and Dijon mustard in a glass measuring cup or mixing bowl. Pour over ribs and continue baking for
another 30 minutes, basting frequently with sauce until nicely
glazed.

Prep = 15 minutes **Cook** = 2½ hours **Yield** = 4 to 6 servings

Braised Lamb Shanks
with Rosemary
and Capers

Working with sour cream is all about timing.
Never bring a liquid that contains sour cream to a boil,
or the sauce will curdle. A note on lamb shanks: Ask the
butcher to crack the lamb shanks so a meat cleaver
or saw is not needed at home.

- 2 lamb shanks, cracked into 3 sections
- 2 tablespoons (30 ml) olive oil
- ¾ teaspoon salt
- 1 cup (240 ml) dry white wine
- 1 bay leaf
- 3 sprigs fresh rosemary
- 2 tablespoons (28 g) butter
- 2 tablespoons (16 g) all-purpose flour
- 1 cup (230 g) sour cream
- 2 tablespoons (18 g) capers, drained

In a heavy skillet, brown lamb shanks in olive oil and transfer to a large casserole. Sprinkle with salt and cover with wine. Add bay leaf and rosemary. Preheat oven to 325°F (170°C, or gas mark 3) and bake for 1½ hours or until tender.

Pour off liquid from pan and strain off fat, reserving about 1 cup (240 ml) liquid. Melt butter in a saucepan and make a roux with flour, stirring with a wire whisk while cooking over medium heat. Blend in liquid, stirring constantly, until smooth and slightly thickened. Blend in sour cream and capers. Heat through but do not boil or sauce will break down. Spoon over lamb shanks.

Prep = 20 minutes   **Cook** = 2 hours   **Yield** = 6 servings

Burgundy Brisket with Caramelized Onions

The marinade has overtones of Beef Bourguignon, with an Asian-inspired accent. Instead of cooking the onions with the brisket, caramelize them separately.

1	cup (240 ml) Burgundy or dry red wine
2	tablespoons (30 ml) soy sauce
1	tablespoon (15 ml) olive oil
1	small onion, grated
2	cloves garlic, crushed
2	stalks celery, sliced
3 to 4	pounds (1.4 to 1.9 kg) beef brisket

CARAMELIZED ONIONS:

3	tablespoons (42 g) butter
2	tablespoons (30 ml) extra-virgin olive oil
2 ½	pounds (1.1 kg) Vidalia onions, sliced
¼	teaspoon salt
¼	teaspoon black pepper
2	tablespoons (26 g) sugar

Combine wine, soy sauce, olive oil, onion, garlic, and celery in a measuring cup. Pierce brisket with a fork and place in a large, heavy-duty resealable freezer bag. Press out excess air and seal. Place in a casserole dish and refrigerate for 4 hours, turning twice.

Preheat oven to 325°F (170°C, or gas mark 3). Remove brisket and place, fat side up, in roasting pan. Cover with half of marinade, reserve remaining marinade. Cover tightly with a lid or heavy foil and bake for 3 hours. Halfway through baking, remove cover, add remaining marinade, return cover, and continue baking until tender. Meanwhile, prepare Caramelized Onions.

For Caramelized Onions: In a large skillet, heat butter and olive oil over medium heat until butter is melted. Add onions, salt, and pepper and sauté, stirring constantly, for about 5 minutes, or until onions start to soften. Add sugar and continue cooking, stirring frequently, until the onions are golden brown, about 20 minutes.

To serve, slice brisket on the diagonal and top with Caramelized Onions.

Prep = 20 minutes   **Cook** = 4 hours   **Yield** = 3 hours

Braised Veal Chops with Chardonnay Reduction

This simple, spur-of-the-moment dinner can
be prepared in about half an hour. The veal chops
are sautéed in one dish and simmered in a reduction
of Chardonnay. If using fresh rosemary, double
the amount given for dried.

1 teaspoon dried sage
1 teaspoon dried rosemary
1 teaspoon salt
1 teaspoon freshly ground pepper
2 cloves garlic, crushed
4 veal chops, about 1 inch (2.5 cm) thick
2 tablespoons (28 g) butter
1 tablespoon (15 ml) olive oil
1 cup (240 ml) Chardonnay or white wine

Make a seasoned rub by combining sage, rosemary, salt, pepper,
and crushed garlic. Rub on both sides of each veal chop. Melt
butter with oil in a large, heavy skillet. Brown chops on both sides,
turning carefully with tongs. Add half of wine, cover, and reduce
heat until chops are tender when pressed with the tip of a knife
(20 to 25 minutes). Transfer chops to a platter and add remaining
wine. Reduce drippings in the pan until syrupy and spoon over
veal chops.

Prep = 15 minutes   **Cook** = 30 to 35 minutes   **Yield** = 4 servings

Steaks Diane

This classic dish used to be prepared tableside in fine restaurants. Now it's back again but often served plated from the kitchen. It can be done either way, and the skillet can be swapped for a copper chafing dish.

2   pounds (905 g) filet of beef
3   tablespoons (42 g) butter
2   tablespoons (30 ml) olive oil
¼   cup (60 ml) brandy or Cognac
¼   cup (40 g) shallots, minced
½   cup (30 g) chopped fresh parsley
1   cup (70 g) sliced mushrooms
1   tablespoon (15 ml) Worcestershire sauce
½   teaspoon Dijon mustard
¼   cup (60 ml) Madeira
    Salt and freshly ground black pepper

Cut beef into ¾-inch (1.9-cm) thick slices. Heat butter and oil in a large nonstick skillet and brown quickly on both sides. Pour brandy over beef and ignite with a match. Let flames burn down and transfer meat to a platter. Pour off all but 2 tablespoons (30 ml) butter and oil. Lower heat and add shallots, parsley, and mushrooms. Sauté until mushrooms are tender. Add Worcestershire sauce, Dijon mustard, and Madeira. Bring to a boil, place beef slices back in the pan, and simmer just for a minute or two to heat through. Arrange steaks on plates and spoon sauce over the top. Season with salt and freshly ground black pepper to taste.

Prep = 15 minutes   **Cook** = 15 minutes   **Yield** = 6 servings

Grilled Pork Chops with Plums and Port Wine

Plums are a wonderful fruit for summer grilling.
This recipe is ideal for an impromptu dinner since there
is little advanced preparation and the pork chops
cook very quickly.

- 6 tablespoons (120 g) plum preserves
- 2 tablespoons (30 ml) port wine
- 2 tablespoons (30 ml) balsamic vinegar
- 1 clove garlic, crushed
- 1 teaspoon salt
- 1 teaspoon pepper
- ½ teaspoon dried rosemary, crushed
- 4 pork chops (about ¾ inch, or 1.9 cm) thick
- 4 plums, pitted and cut into wedges

Preheat grill. Combine 4 tablespoons (80 g) plum preserves, port wine, balsamic vinegar, garlic, ¼ teaspoon salt, and ¼ teaspoon pepper. Mix rosemary with remaining salt and pepper. Sprinkle rosemary mixture on both sides of pork chops. Grill chops, turning once and brushing both sides of pork chops with preserves mixture, for about 5 minutes per side, or until no longer pink near the bone. Melt remaining preserves and brush on plums, grill for 3 minutes per side.

Prep = 15 minutes   **Cook** = 16 to 20 minutes   **Yield** = 4 servings

Harvest Veal and Apple Skewers

Deep, dark Oloroso sherry creates a rich glaze.
These kebabs can also be made with pork. Both veal
and pork are enhanced by the fruity sherry with
apple juice and ginger.

- ¾ cup (175 ml) Oloroso sherry
- ¾ cup apple juice concentrate (undiluted)
- 3 tablespoons (45 ml) olive oil
- 2 teaspoons soy sauce
- ¼ teaspoon ground ginger
- 1 ½ pounds (680 g) veal, cut into 16 cubes
- 1 medium red onion, cut into 8 wedges
- 1 Granny Smith apple, cut into 8 wedges

HARVEST GLAZE:
- ¾ cup (240 g) apricot jam
- 2 tablespoons (30 ml) Oloroso sherry
- 2 tablespoons (30 ml) apple cider vinegar
- 2 tablespoons (32 g) tomato paste
- ⅛ teaspoon ground ginger

Combine sherry, apple juice, 1 tablespoon (15 ml) olive oil, soy sauce, and ginger in a medium bowl and add veal cubes. Stir to coat. Cover and refrigerate at least 4 hours, stirring twice. Heat grill to medium-high. On 4 metal skewers, thread veal cubes, with 2 onion and apple wedges on each. Use remaining 2 tablespoons (30 ml) olive oil to brush kebabs and lightly oil grates.

Place skewers on grill and cook, turning occasionally, until grill marks are visible, about 8 minutes. Start basting with glaze and continue cooking for 4 to 8 minutes more, turning frequently so as not to burn. Veal should be nicely glazed and no longer pink inside.

For Harvest Glaze: Combine apricot jam, sherry, vinegar, tomato paste, and ginger in a glass measuring cup. Heat for 1 minute in the microwave.

Prep = 20 minutes **Chill** = 4 hours **Cook** = 20 minutes
Yield = 4 servings

Kansas City Skillet Steak with Merlot and Plum Tomato Salsa

Kansas City, Missouri, is the steak and
barbecue capital of the world. That doesn't mean,
though, that every cut of meat is char-grilled or hickory
smoked. This pan-sautéed version is a good choice when
outdoor cooking—and the requisite fending off
of mosquitoes—isn't an option.

4 Kansas City steaks (8 ounces, or 225 g, each),
¾ to 1 inch (1.9 to 2.5 cm) thick
1 cup (240 ml) Merlot
2 teaspoons (10 ml) soy sauce
1 clove garlic, crushed
3 tablespoons (45 ml) olive oil
Salt and pepper
7 large plum tomatoes
6 scallions, sliced
2 tablespoons (30 ml) balsamic vinegar

Pierce steaks with a fork. Arrange in a baking dish or casserole.
Combine Merlot, soy sauce, garlic, 2 tablespoons (30 ml) olive oil,
and salt and pepper. Cover and marinate for 3 to 4 hours in the
refrigerator, turning twice.

Meanwhile, blanch plum tomatoes by placing in a bowl and
covering with boiling water. Allow to stand for about 2 minutes,
or until the skins start to split. Drain and remove peels, scoop out
seeds, and dice. Combine with scallions.

Heat remaining olive oil in a large, heavy skillet. Remove steaks
from marinade. For medium rare, sauté over medium-high heat
for about 3 minutes each side. Remove steaks to a platter. Add
balsamic vinegar to deglaze pan, then add tomatoes and scallions,
stirring briefly to warm through, but do not overcook. Spoon over
steaks.

Prep = 20 minutes **Chill** = 3 to 4 hours **Cook** = 10 minutes
Yield = 4 servings

Herbed Roast Leg of Lamb with Wine Reduction

Leg of lamb is a spring holiday tradition. The boneless version is much easier to carve, especially for a buffet. The rosemary and red wine reduction creates a wonderful aroma while the lamb is roasting.

1   tablespoon (4 g) fresh chopped rosemary leaves
1   tablespoon (4 g) fresh thyme
¼   cup (16 g) finely chopped fresh parsley
3   tablespoons (45 ml) olive oil
2   teaspoons kosher salt
½   teaspoon pepper
2   cloves garlic, crushed
6   pounds (2.7 kg) boneless leg of lamb, tied with string
2   cups (475 ml) red wine
2   tablespoons (8 g) snipped fresh chives

Preheat oven to 325°F (170°C, or gas mark 3). In a small bowl, combine rosemary, thyme, parsley, olive oil, salt, pepper, and garlic. Spread herb mixture over the entire surface of lamb. Insert oven thermometer through the thickest part of the meat, taking care that it does not rest on fat. Bake, uncovered, for 2 hours and 10 to 15 minutes for medium rare, or until thermometer reads 140°F (60°C). For medium, bake until thermometer reads 155°F (68°C).

Transfer lamb to a serving platter and tent with foil. Letting the meat "rest" will raise the temperatures by 5 more degrees.

Meanwhile, add wine to pan and heat to deglaze the pan, scraping up the browned bits from the bottom. When thoroughly dissolved, transfer to a saucepan and boil vigorously to reduce by two-thirds, or until you have a syrupy glaze. Add chives. Serve in a sauceboat alongside lamb.

Prep = 15 minutes   **Cook** = 2½ hours   **Yield** = 10 to 12 servings

Madeira Glazed Ham

There are innumerable methods for glazing a
baked ham, from pineapple rings with brown sugar
and cherries to pouring a bottle of cola over the top.
A colonial tavern in Virginia serves this
Madeira-glazed ham for Easter dinner.

1   cup (225 g) firmly packed brown sugar
2   tablespoons (28 g) butter
⅔   cup (160 ml) maple syrup
½   cup (120 ml) Madeira wine
½   teaspoon dry mustard
½   teaspoon ground cinnamon
¼   teaspoon ground ginger
1   fully cooked smoked bone-in ham (6 to 8 pounds, or 2.7 to 3.6 kg)
    Whole cloves

Combine brown sugar, butter, maple syrup, wine, dry mustard, cinnamon, and ginger in a medium saucepan. Bring to a boil, reduce
heat, and simmer until slightly thickened (about 5 minutes).

Preheat oven to 325°F (170°C, or gas mark 3). Line a shallow
roasting pan with nonstick aluminum foil. Place ham, cut side
down, on the rack in the pan. Insert a meat thermometer into the
thickest part of ham (avoid resting it against fat). Score across fat
on the diagonal to create a diamond-shaped crosshatched effect.
Insert cloves where cuts intersect. Bake, uncovered, for 1 hour and
30 minutes, or until the thermometer reads 140°F (60°C). During
the last half hour of baking, bush ham twice with glaze.

Let ham rest, loosely tented with foil, on a serving platter, for
easier carving. Lightly brush with additional glaze before bringing
to the table, and serve remaining glaze in a sauceboat.

Prep = 10 minutes   **Cook** = 1½ hours   **Yield** = 20 servings

Medallions of Pork Normande

These medallions can also be made from boneless pork chops. The landmark Harborview restaurant in Stonington, Connecticut, featured this specialty. Countless guests still remember its water view and the pork tenderloin in a sauce of apples and cream.

4   pork tenderloin filets
1   tablespoon (8 g) all-purpose flour
2   tablespoons (28 g) butter
    Salt
4   baby leeks, washed thoroughly to remove sand and sliced thinly
½   teaspoon whole mustard seeds
⅔   cup (160 ml) dry white wine
2   small, firm apples, peeled, cored, and sliced
⅔   cup (160 ml) heavy cream

Dredge pork in flour. Melt butter in a medium skillet over medium-high heat. Add pork, salt lightly, and sauté on both sides until browned. Add leeks to the pan and cook for 3 minutes. Stir in mustard seeds, pour in wine, and simmer for 10 minutes, turning pork several times. Add apple slices and cream. Simmer for about another 3 minutes, or until sauce is slightly thickened.

Prep = 15 minutes   **Cook** = 25 minutes   **Yield** = 4 servings

Prime Rib with Yorkshire Pudding and Portobello Mushroom Marsala Gravy

Yorkshire pudding is simply a big popover baked in a casserole dish. The decadent part is that it is made with prime rib drippings.

1	rib roast (4 to 6 pounds, or 1.9 to 2.7 kg)
1	clove garlic, crushed
½	teaspoon salt
¼	teaspoon pepper
¾	cup Marsala wine
1 ¼	cups (295 ml) beef broth
5	tablespoons (70 g) butter
2	portobello mushroom caps, sliced
1	shallot, minced
3	tablespoons (24 g) all-purpose flour

YORKSHIRE PUDDING:

	Reserved drippings
	Vegetable oil
1	cup (125 g) all-purpose flour
1	cup (240 ml) milk
½	teaspoon salt
2	eggs

Prep = 25 minutes   **Cook** = 2¼ to 3¼ hours   **Yield** = 8 servings

Preheat oven to 350°F (180°C, or gas mark 4). Line a shallow roasting pan with foil. Place roast, fat side up, in pan. Score fat and rub the surface with garlic. Sprinkle with salt and pepper. Insert a meat thermometer into the thickest part of the roast, being sure that it's not resting on the fat.

For medium rare, roast for 1 hour and 45 minutes to 2 hours and 15 minutes, or until thermometer reads 135°F (57°C). For medium, add another 30 minutes to the roasting time, or until the thermometer reads 150°F (66°C). Transfer roast to a platter and tent loosely with foil. This allows the meat to rest and raises the internal temperature by 10 degrees.

Pour drippings into a 1-cup (240 ml) glass measuring cup and reserve for the Yorkshire Pudding.

Pour Marsala wine and beef broth into the roasting pan and set on stove-top burner. Heat to deglaze pan, scraping bits from the bottom with a wooden spoon until dissolved. Pour liquid into a 1-quart (945-ml) glass measuring cup. In a medium saucepan, melt butter and sauté mushrooms and shallot until tender (about 5 minutes). Sprinkle with flour and blend in until smooth. Blend in broth mixture and cook, stirring constantly, until thickened. Serve with Yorkshire Pudding.

For Yorkshire Pudding: Preheat oven to 450°F (230°C, or gas mark 8). Measure drippings and if they don't amount to ¼ cup (60 ml), add oil until they do. Pour into a 9-inch (22.9-cm) square pan. Beat flour, milk, salt, and eggs with a wire whisk, just until smooth. Heat pan for about 3 minutes in the oven. Carefully remove from oven and pour batter over drippings. Bake for 18 to 23 minutes, or until puffy and golden brown (pudding will deflate). Cut into squares and serve with sliced prime rib and gravy.

Mom's Madeira Meatloaf with Cremini Gravy

Admittedly, Mom did not originally put wine in her meatloaf, but it was tweaked a little for this book. The cold slices of the Madeira version are nearly rugged pâté. When served, hot mashed potatoes and gravy are a must.

½ cup (60 g) herb-seasoned stuffing, crushed finely
1 cup (240 ml) Madeira
1 ½ pounds (680 g) very lean ground beef
¼ cup (40 g) minced onion
1 clove garlic, crushed
½ teaspoon salt
¼ teaspoon cracked pepper
1 teaspoon Worcestershire sauce
1 large egg

CREMINI GRAVY:
1 cup (70 g) chopped cremini or portobello mushrooms
1 tablespoon (14 g) butter
¼ cup (60 ml) Madeira
1 envelope (1 ounce, or 28 g) mushroom gravy mix

Preheat oven 350°F (180°C, or gas mark 4). In a large mixing bowl, combine stuffing with 1 cup (240 ml) Madeira to moisten. Mix in ground beef, onion, garlic, salt, pepper, Worcestershire sauce, and egg. Spread mixture into an ungreased 9 × 5-inch (22.5 × 13-cm) loaf pan. Bake for 1 hour and 15 minutes. Let stand for 5 minutes before removing from pan. Slice and serve with Cremini Gravy.

For Cremini Gravy: In a small saucepan, sauté mushrooms in butter until most of the moisture has evaporated and mushrooms are tender. In a glass measuring cup, substitute ¼ cup (60 ml) Madeira for part of the water in the gravy mix directions. Blend in dry mix. Add to mushrooms in pan and heat through, stirring constantly until gravy is smooth and thickened.

Prep = 20 minutes   **Cook** = 1½ hours   **Yield** = 6 servings

Raisin Bread Stuffed Pork Chops with Sherry

This entrée is a great use for those pieces of bread remaining in the bag from a week's worth of morning raisin toast. French or sourdough bread will also complement the recipe.

4   slices raisin bread
1   small apple, cored and cut into cubes
3   tablespoons (42 g) butter
6   tablespoons (90 ml) sherry
4   boneless pork chops, about 1 inch (2.5 cm) thick
    Salt and pepper
2   tablespoons (30 g) brown sugar mixed with 1 teaspoon dried marjoram

Cut raisin bread into cubes and set aside. In a small skillet, sauté apple in 2 tablespoons (28 g) butter until lightly browned. Remove from heat and stir in raisin bread and 2 tablespoons (30 ml) sherry. With a sharp paring knife, cut a deep pocket into the side of each pork chop. Stuff pork chops with stuffing.

Preheat oven to 350°F (180°C, or gas mark 4). Use remaining tablespoon (14 g) of butter to grease a 9-inch (22.5-cm) square baking dish. Place pork chops in dish and cover with 4 table-spoons (60 ml) sherry. Sprinkle pork chops lightly with salt and pepper, followed by the brown sugar mixture. Cover tightly with foil and bake for 45 minutes. Remove foil and bake for 45 minutes longer, or until pork chops are nicely glazed.

Prep = 20 minutes   **Cook** = 1 hour, 35 minutes   **Yield** = 4 servings

Slow-Cooker Swiss Steak with Rosemary and Red Wine

Swiss steak is much more of an American nostalgia dish than a European classic. That's why it appears in this section, although the addition of rosemary and red wine contributes to a Continental flavor. The slow cooker makes it easier to prepare than using a Dutch oven.

- 1½ pounds boneless chuck steak, about ¾ inch (1.9 cm) thick
- 3 tablespoons (24 g) all-purpose flour
- ½ teaspoon dry mustard
- ½ teaspoon salt
- 2 tablespoons (30 ml) olive oil
- 1 can (14.5 ounces, or 411 g) whole tomatoes, drained
- 1 onion, sliced
- 1 tablespoon (4 g) minced fresh rosemary
- 2 cloves garlic, crushed
- 1 large green bell pepper, seeded and sliced
- 1 cup (240 ml) dry red wine
- 1 teaspoon Worcestershire sauce

Cut chuck steak into 6 smaller steaks. In a small bowl, mix flour, mustard, and salt. Dredge beef in flour mixture. Heat oil in a medium skillet over medium heat and brown beef on both sides (turning at least once) for a total of 15 minutes. Place beef in slow cooker. Cover with tomatoes, sliced onion, rosemary, garlic, and bell pepper. Combine red wine with Worcestershire sauce and pour over beef and vegetables. Cover and set slow cooker on low for 7 to 9 hours, or until meat is tender and sauce is slightly thickened.

Prep = 10 minutes   **Cook** = 7 to 9 hours   **Yield** = 6 servings

Sweet & Saucy Country-Style Ribs in Port

These oven-baked ribs are a favorite do-ahead recipe for company. They don't require last-minute grilling or taking them outside to the barbecue. For this reason, consider them "winter ribs" since they never have to be grilled outside.

3   pounds (1.4 kg) country-style pork ribs
    Salt and pepper
1   cup (275 g) chili sauce
⅓   cup (80 ml) port wine
¼   cup (60 g) steak sauce
¾   cup (240 g) grape jelly

Preheat oven to 350°F (180°C, or gas mark 4). Place ribs in a 9 × 13-inch (22.5 × 32.5-inch) pan. Lightly sprinkle with salt and pepper. Cover and bake for 2 hours. Drain off all of the fat. Combine chili sauce, port wine, steak sauce, and jelly until heated through. Pour over ribs and continue baking for another 30 minutes, basting frequently with sauce until nicely glazed.

Prep = 10 minutes   **Cook** = 2½ hours   **Yield** = 6 servings

Venison with Lingonberry Wine Sauce

Venison is usually considered deer meat, but it can
also be from game such as caribou, elk, or moose.
Lingonberries are popular in Sweden and appear in
Austrian and Swiss dishes, as well. Cranberry
preserves may be substituted.

6	venison steaks, about 6 ounces (165 g) each
	Salt and pepper
¾	cup (230 ml) dry red wine
1	tablespoon (15 g) Dijon mustard
1	tablespoon (14 g) butter
1	tablespoon (15 ml) extra-virgin olive oil
¾	cup (175 ml) beef broth
½	cup (160 g) lingonberry preserves
¼	cup (40 g) dried currants
½	cup (50 g) sliced scallions

Season steaks with salt and pepper. Combine wine and mustard.
Place steaks in a shallow glass dish, and pour marinade over
meat. Refrigerate for 2 to 4 hours.

Remove venison from marinade, reserving remaining marinade.
In a large skillet, heat butter and olive oil over medium heat until
butter is melted. Place venison steaks in skillet, cooking about 3
minutes on each side. Add beef broth and simmer 10 minutes, but
do not overcook or venison may be tough.

Remove venison to platter and keep warm. Pour reserved marinade into saucepan, and add lingonberry preserves, currants, and
scallions. Deglaze pan, reducing mixture until syrupy. Spoon over
venison steaks and serve.

Prep = 10 minutes   **Chill** = 2 to 4 hours   **Cook** = 30 minutes
Yield = 6 servings

Poultry

Arroz con Pollo

There are enough versions of
arroz con pollo to fill an entire book. Chiles can be
added with the bell peppers for extra heat.

4 chicken drumsticks

4 chicken thighs

½ teaspoon salt

½ teaspoon fresh black pepper

1 tablespoon (15 ml) olive oil

1 small onion, chopped

2 cloves garlic, crushed

1 medium red bell pepper, seeded and chopped

1 medium green bell pepper, seeded and chopped

2 ounces (55 g) smoked ham

1 ⅓ cups (240 g) canned tomatoes, drained and chopped

1 tablespoon (16 g) tomato paste

2 teaspoons (4 g) adobo seasoning

1 cup (240 ml) low-sodium chicken broth

1 cup (240 ml) white wine

1 cup (185 g) uncooked long-grain rice

3 tablespoons (12 g) minced fresh cilantro

½ cup (65 g) frozen peas, thawed

Season chicken with salt and pepper. In a large skillet, heat oil over medium-high heat, brown chicken on all sides for about 8 minutes. Transfer chicken to a platter and pour off all but about 2 tablespoons (30 ml) fat from the pan.

Reduce heat to low. Add onion and garlic and sauté, stirring until onions are soft (about 2 minutes). Add bell peppers and diced ham and continue cooking and stirring until they begin to soften (about 3 minutes). Add tomatoes, tomato paste, adobo seasoning, broth, wine, and rice. Simmer over low heat with skillet partially covered (set lid slightly off center so some steam can escape from the side), until chicken and rice are done, 25 to 35 minutes. Stir in cilantro and peas.

Prep = 15 minutes **Cook** = 45 minutes **Yield** = 8 servings

Burgundy-Balsamic Chicken Breasts

Tart balsamic vinegar and wine make a great reduction sauce for chicken. Even though this is not a true salad, consider serving the dish on a nest of field greens, drizzled with the glaze.

4   boneless, skinless chicken breast halves
    Salt and pepper
¼   cup (31 g) all-purpose flour
1   tablespoon (14 g) butter
2   tablespoons (30 ml) olive oil
8   ounces (225 g) porcini mushrooms, sliced
2   cloves garlic, crushed
¼   cup (60 ml) balsamic vinegar
1   cup (240 ml) Burgundy or other red wine

Lightly sprinkle chicken with salt and pepper. Place in a resealable plastic bag with flour and shake. Remove from bag and shake off any excess flour. Melt butter and olive oil in a large nonstick skillet. Cook chicken breasts for 3 minutes on one side until browned. Turn chicken breasts over and brown for 3 minutes on other side. Transfer to a platter. Add mushrooms and garlic to drippings. Sauté until tender, about 5 minutes. Return chicken breasts to the pan along with vinegar and wine. Reduce liquid to half until it becomes syrupy. Spoon balsamic glaze with mushrooms over chicken breasts.

Prep = 15 minutes   **Cook** = 18 minutes   **Yield** = 4 servings

Buttermilk Fried Chicken with Wine Country Gravy

Old-fashioned skillet-fried chicken is very different
from what is available in most establishments. The
coating is merely seasoned flour, and it's cooked slowly
on the stove top instead of in a deep fryer. The crust
on the bottom of the skillet is used in a creamy
gravy that is delightful with mashed potatoes.

1 cup (125 g) plus 3 tablespoons (24 g) all-purpose flour
1 tablespoon paprika
1 ½ teaspoons salt
½ teaspoon pepper
3 pounds (1.4 kg) chicken, cut up
1 cup (240 ml) buttermilk
Vegetable oil
1 tablespoon (14 g) butter
1 cup (240 ml) half-and-half
1 cup (240 ml) dry white wine

In a shallow dish, mix 1 cup (125 g) flour, paprika, salt, and pepper.
Put buttermilk in a bowl, then dip chicken into buttermilk and coat
with flour. Pour ¼ inch (6 mm) oil into a skillet and heat over
medium-high heat. Cook chicken in oil, skin side down, for about
10 minutes or until lightly browned on all sides; reduce heat to low
and turn chicken skin-side up.

Simmer, uncovered, for 20 minutes, or until the juice of chicken
is clear when cut through the thickest piece. Transfer chicken to a
warm serving platter. Remove pan from heat. Cool slightly and
pour off all but 2 tablespoons (30 ml) of drippings. Return to heat
and add butter. Blend in 3 tablespoons (24 g) flour; cook until
smooth and bubbling, then blend in half-and-half and wine, stirring until thickened and smooth.

Season with salt and pepper to taste. If gravy gets too thick,
you can always thin it down with a little extra half-and-half
or wine.

Prep = 15 minutes   **Cook** = 40 minutes   **Yield** = 6 servings

Coq au Vin Rouge
Casa Grimaldi

Singer, actor, and producer Franco Grimaldi also
creates designer show houses. Franco, while working
in a Connecticut neighborhood, shared his favorite
dish during the writing of this book.

3   pounds (1.4 kg) chicken, cut up
    All-purpose flour, for dredging
1   stick (¼ pound, or 112 g) butter
    Salt and pepper
2   ounces (60 ml) Cognac
    bouquet garni*
3   cups (710 ml) red wine
3   medium onions, sliced
2   cloves garlic, crushed
12 medium to large mushrooms, sliced
    Parsley sprigs, for garnish

Dredge chicken in a shallow dish of flour by rolling pieces in it
until well coated. Melt 5 tablespoons (70 g) butter in a large nonstick skillet with cover and brown chicken on all sides for about 15
minutes. When done, sprinkle with salt and pepper. Add Cognac
and allow it to warm up in pan; then ignite it with a match. When
flames die down, add bouquet garni and pour wine over chicken.
Cover; simmer for 45 minutes. About 15 minutes before chicken is
done, melt remaining butter in a saucepan and sauté onions
and garlic over low heat for 5 minutes. Add mushrooms and continue
to sauté over low heat for another 10 minutes, until tender.
Arrange chicken pieces on a platter. Spoon mushrooms and
onions over chicken. Remove bouquet garni and strain pan liquid
over chicken. Franco traditionally serves this dish with wild rice
and a seasonal vegetable.

*For bouquet garni: Combine 2 tablespoons (12 g) chopped celery,
a sprig of parsley, ⅛ teaspoon thyme, and 1 bay leaf in a piece of
cheesecloth and tie into a small bag.

Prep = 20 minutes   **Cook** = 1 hour, 10 minutes   **Yield** = 4 servings

Duck Jambalaya

Ducks are typically served in halves, so
sometimes there will be a spare, especially after serving
duck to an odd number of dinner guests.
This recipe is a perfect use for it.

¼ cup (50 g) duck fat, reserved from roasting
2 cups (300 g) sliced turkey sausage
1 cup (160 g) chopped onion
¾ cup (113 g) diced and seeded green bell pepper
1 clove garlic, crushed
½ cup (75 g) chopped Tasso ham (optional)*
½ cup (120 ml) dry white wine
1 can (16 ounces, or 455 g) tomatoes, undrained
1 teaspoon salt
½ teaspoon dried thyme
½ teaspoon dried basil
¼ teaspoon dried marjoram
¼ teaspoon paprika
¼ teaspoon red pepper sauce
2 tablespoons (8 g) chopped fresh parsley
1 cup (185 g) uncooked converted long-grain rice
2 cups (280 g) chopped duck meat

In a large stockpot, melt duck fat and sauté turkey sausage until browned, then remove with a slotted spoon. Add onion, bell pepper, and garlic, and continue sautéing until tender (about 5 minutes). Stir in sausage, ham, wine, tomatoes with their liquid, salt, thyme, basil, marjoram, paprika, pepper sauce, parsley, rice, and duck meat. Bring to a boil, reduce heat, and simmer for 25 minutes.

*Tasso ham is a staple of Cajun cuisine but it's actually smoked pork shoulder. This ingredient is often available now in markets around the country. If you can't find it, simply substitute traditional ham.

Prep = 20 minutes   **Cook** = 40 to 45 minutes   **Yield** = 6 servings

Easy Turkey and Madeira Pot Pie

Need to pull together a from-scratch, family-style dinner in little or no time? Here's the answer. This is the kind of recipe that simply requires a little help from convenience foods—often that's the best kind!

Large baking potato, baked then chilled
1 tablespoon (14 g) butter
¼ cup (40 g) minced onion
½ cup (50 g) sliced celery
1 jar (10 ounces, or 285 ml) turkey gravy
⅓ cup (80 ml) Madeira
1 package (10 ounces, or 280 g) frozen mixed vegetables
2 cups (280 g) cubed white-meat turkey
¼ teaspoon pepper
¼ teaspoon marjoram
1 can (8-count, standard size) refrigerated biscuits

Preheat oven to 400°F (200°C, or gas mark 6). Cut potato into ½-inch (1.3-cm) cubes. In a medium nonstick skillet, melt butter over medium heat and sauté onion and celery in butter until tender (about 3 minutes). Stir in gravy, Madeira, vegetables, turkey, pepper, and marjoram. Bring to boil, cook for 2 minutes, then remove from heat. Pour into a 2-quart (1.9-L) casserole. Arrange biscuits on top of casserole and bake for 12 to 14 minutes, or until biscuits are golden brown.

Prep = 10 minutes   **Cook** = 20 minutes   **Yield** = 6 servings

Hazelnut Chicken in Champagne Frangelico Sauce

A favorite dish from a Rhode Island inn inspired this recipe. The original version features oranges in the sauce, but this Champagne version isn't quite as sweet.

- 4 boneless, skinless chicken breast halves
- ½ cup (60 g) dry bread crumbs
- ½ cup (58 g) chopped hazelnuts
- ¼ teaspoon dried thyme
- Pinch of salt
- 1 egg, lightly beaten with 1 tablespoon (15 ml) water
- All-purpose flour, for dredging
- ¼ cup (55 g) butter
- 1 cup (240 ml) heavy cream
- ½ cup (120 ml) Champagne
- 2 tablespoons (30 ml) Frangelico liqueur

Flatten chicken breasts slightly by lightly pounding. Combine bread crumbs, hazelnuts, thyme, and salt in a shallow dish. Put egg wash in a shallow bowl. Dredge chicken fillets in flour; dip in egg wash and coat with crumb mixture, shaking off excess crumbs.

Melt butter in a large nonstick skillet over medium heat. Cook chicken until golden brown on both sides for a total of 15 minutes. Transfer to a platter and keep in a warm oven while preparing sauce. Pour cream, Champagne, and Frangelico liqueur into pan drippings. Deglaze pan, allowing sauce to reduce until slightly thickened. Serve over chicken.

Prep = 15 minutes   **Cook** = 25 minutes   **Yield** = 4 servings

Currant-Glazed Cornish Hens with Carrot and Turnip Purée

Cornish hen recipes are more popular in the United Kingdom than in the United States, as are currants. In English and Irish cookbooks, currants are used more frequently and in place of raisins. They are a wonderful accent to pork and poultry dishes.

2   Cornish game hens
     Cracked black pepper
8   slices bacon

CURRANT GLAZE:
1   cup (240 ml) chicken stock
½   cup (120 ml) port wine
1   cup (240 ml) dry red wine
⅔   cup (100 g) dried currants
1   tablespoon (15 ml) balsamic vinegar
⅔   cup (213 g) red currant jelly

CARROT AND TURNIP PURÉE:
2   pounds (905 g) carrots, peeled and cut into 1-inch (2.5-cm) lengths
2   pounds (905 g) turnips, peeled and cut into 1-inch (2.5-cm) lengths
¼   teaspoon ground ginger
½   cup (115 g) sour cream
4   tablespoons (55 g) softened butter
     Salt and pepper

Prep = 30 minutes   **Cook** = 2 hours   **Yield** = 4 servings

Wash Cornish hens, pat dry, and split in half. Place, skin side up, in a baking pan and sprinkle with pepper. Cover hens with bacon slices. Preheat oven to 400°F (200°C, or gas mark 6) and bake for 15 minutes, then reduce oven temperature to 350°F (180°C, or gas mark 4) and bake 40 to 45 minutes, until skin is crisp. Remove from oven and discard bacon. Spoon glaze over hens and serve with Carrot and Turnip Purée.

For Currant Glaze: Bring chicken stock, port, and red wine to a boil and reduce by half. Add currants, vinegar, and jelly. Boil until glaze is syrupy enough to coat a spoon.

For Carrot and Turnip Purée: Cook carrots and turnips in boiling, salted water for 30 to 40 minutes or until tender. Drain well. Purée in food processor with ginger. Add sour cream and butter, and purée until blended. Season with salt and pepper to taste.

Old-Fashioned Chicken à la King

Chicken à la King has been the butt of many bad banquet-food jokes. However, when properly prepared, it's a nostalgic dish that really hits the spot and makes a great luncheon entrée.

5	tablespoons (70 g) butter
1	cup (70 g) sliced mushrooms
1	shallot, minced
1	medium red bell pepper, seeded and chopped
¼	cup (31 g) all-purpose flour
1	cup (240 ml) chicken stock
1	cup (240 ml) half-and-half
¼	cup (60 ml) sherry
1	tablespoon (4 g) snipped fresh chives
3	cups (420 g) cubed cooked chicken
½	cup (65 g) petite frozen peas, thawed
	Salt and pepper
4	baked puff pastry shells

Melt 1 tablespoon (14 g) butter in a medium nonstick saucepan over medium heat. Sauté mushrooms and shallot until tender, for about 5 minutes. In another saucepan, cook bell pepper in boiling water for 3 minutes. Rinse under cold water, drain well, and pat dry.

In a medium saucepan over medium heat, melt remaining 4 tablespoons (55 g) butter and blend in flour with a wire whisk. Cook for about 1 minute, until smooth and bubbling. Slowly blend in chicken stock, half-and-half, and sherry. Cook, whisking constantly, until sauce thickens and boils. Stir in chives, chicken, and peas. Season with salt and pepper to taste and serve in warmed puff pastry shells.

Prep = 15 minutes   **Cook** = 20 minutes
Yield = 4 servings

Potato Chip Chicken Chardonnay

Legend has it that this recipe originated from
Lily Pulitzer, the lady behind the pink-and-green revolution.
Back in the days when chintz pants tended to match the
draperies, this oven-fried chicken dish was all the rage.

- 1   cup (240 ml) lime juice
- 1   teaspoon salt
- 1   teaspoon ground black pepper
- 1 ½ cups (355 ml) Chardonnay or white wine
- 4   cloves garlic, crushed
- 1   teaspoon dried thyme
- 1   teaspoon dried basil
- 3   broiler chickens, quartered
- 2   sticks (½ pound, or 225 g) butter, melted
- 3   cups (345 g) crushed potato chips

In a large bowl, combine juice, salt, pepper, wine, garlic, thyme,
and basil. Add chicken pieces, cover, and marinate in the
refrigerator for 4 hours, turning every hour.

Preheat oven to 450°F (230°C, or gas mark 8). Dip each
chicken piece in melted butter, then roll in crushed potato chips.
Arrange chicken in a large, shallow baking dish and bake,
uncovered, for 1 hour.

Prep = 15 minutes   **Chill** = 4 hours   **Cook** = 1 hour
Yield = 6 servings

Pan-Seared Duck Breasts with Raspberry Merlot Glaze

Duck breast is usually prepared in a different manner from a crispy roasted duck. The meat resembles a medium-rare steak when sliced. Both presentations are good; however, preparing duck breast takes much less time and effort.

4   boneless duck breasts (6 ounces, or 170 g, each)
1   teaspoon salt
4   shallots, minced
⅓   cup (80 ml) Merlot
½   cup (160 g) seedless black raspberry jam
¼   cup (60 ml) red wine vinegar
1   cup (125 g) fresh raspberries

Preheat oven to 350°F (180°C, or gas mark 4). Line a baking sheet with nonstick aluminum foil. Make 3 slashes across the skin of each duck breast at a 45 degree angle and sprinkle with salt. Heat a medium nonstick skillet over high heat. When pan is hot, place duck breasts, skin side down in it, and cook for about 5 minutes or until skin is brown and crispy. Flip over and cook for 2 more minutes. Transfer duck breasts, skin side up, to baking sheet.

Carefully discard all but 2 tablespoons (30 ml) duck fat. Sauté shallots in pan until they begin to turn golden, about 3 minutes. Add Merlot and stir with a wooden spoon to loosen any browned bits of duck. Add jam and vinegar, and boil for about 3 minutes, stirring occasionally. Meanwhile, place baking sheet in oven and cook duck for 6 minutes.

Remove from oven and slice each breast on the diagonal in ¼-inch (6-mm) strips. Arrange in a fanlike pattern on warmed plates. Stir raspberries into warm glaze and spoon over duck.

Prep = 15 minutes   **Cook** = 20 minutes   **Yield** = 4 servings

Pulled Turkey
with Port Wine

This is a nice holiday version of pulled turkey
to serve to a gathering of friends. Using the slow
cooker makes it simple to put together on a busy day.
Just put all of the ingredients in the slow cooker and
forget about them while preparing the house
for guests and running errands.

 1 bone-in, skinless turkey breast (5½ pounds, or 2.5 kg)
 ½ cup (75 g) chopped and seeded green bell pepper
 1 cup (160 g) chopped onion
 ½ cup (120 ml) chili sauce
 2 tablespoons (30 ml) red wine vinegar
 1 tablespoon (15 g) brown sugar
 ¼ cup (60 ml) port wine
 1 teaspoon Worcestershire sauce
12 club rolls or sandwich buns

Place turkey, green bell pepper, and onion in a slow cooker.
Combine chili sauce, vinegar, brown sugar, port, and
Worcestershire sauce and pour over turkey. Cover and cook on
low for 5 to 6 hours, or until turkey begins to fall apart.

Remove turkey from cooking liquid (reserving liquid) and shred
apart with a fork. Return turkey to liquid and mix together. Split
open warm club rolls and fill with shredded turkey.

Prep = 10 minutes   **Cook** = 5 to 6 hours   **Yield** = 12 servings

Port Wine and Cranberry-Braised Turkey Breast

This is one of those simple slow-cooker recipes for a busy day. It can be served with some of usual turkey trimmings like mashed sweet potatoes or creamed peas with pearl onions. It's like having Thanksgiving without all of the fuss.

1   whole skinless turkey breast (3 to 4 pounds, or 1.4 to 1.9 kg)
1   can (15 ounces, or 420 g) whole-berry cranberry sauce
1   envelope low-sodium onion soup mix
½   cup (120 ml) port wine
2   tablespoons (36 g) orange juice concentrate

Place turkey in slow cooker. Combine cranberry sauce, onion soup mix, port wine, and orange juice concentrate. Pour over turkey and cook on low for 6 to 8 hours. Transfer to a platter and served sliced with cranberry glaze

Prep = 10 minutes   **Cook** = 6 to 8 hours   **Yield** = 6 servings

Rosemary Chicken Chardonnay

If you have fresh rosemary on hand, you can simmer a sprig of it with the chicken and then remove before serving. As always, when working with sour cream in a sauce, blend it into very hot liquid but do not bring the sour cream to a boil or it could break down and separate.

- 6 boneless, skinless chicken breasts
  Salt and pepper
- 4 tablespoons (55 g) butter
- ¾ cup (75 g) sliced scallions
- 8 ounces (225 g) sliced mushrooms
- 1 cup (240 ml) Chardonnay or white wine
- ¼ teaspoon dried thyme
- ½ teaspoon dried rosemary
- 1 cup (230 g) sour cream

Season chicken breasts with salt and pepper. Melt butter in a large skillet and brown chicken breasts on all sides. Remove when browned and set aside on a platter. Add scallions and mushrooms to the skillet and sauté until mushrooms are tender. Add chicken, wine, thyme, and rosemary. Cover and simmer over low heat for 30 minutes. Transfer chicken to a platter and keep warm. Reduce juices in the pan to about ¼ cup (60 ml). Blend in sour cream and stir until melted and just heated through (do not allow to boil). Pour over chicken breasts.

Prep = 15 minutes **Cook** = 45 to 50 minutes
Yield = 6 servings

Sesame-Sherry Chicken

Everyone needs recipes for oven-baked chicken because no one really wants to tackle frying most of the time and takeout is . . . well, takeout. This version with sesame seeds and sherry can become part of a regular repertoire.

1   fryer (3 pounds, or 1.4 kg), cut up
1   teaspoon herb-seasoned salt
½   cup (120 ml) buttermilk
1   teaspoon Worcestershire sauce
½   cup (120 ml) sherry
1   clove garlic, crushed
¾   cup (90 g) unseasoned dry bread crumbs
¾   cup (108 g) toasted sesame seeds*
¼   cup (16 g) minced flat-leaf parsley
⅓   cup (75 g) butter, melted

Arrange chicken in a bowl just large enough to hold it. Sprinkle with seasoned salt. Blend together buttermilk, Worcestershire sauce, sherry, and garlic. Marinate in refrigerator for 4 hours, turning two or three times.

Preheat oven to 350°F (180°C, or gas mark 4). In a small bowl, stir together bread crumbs, sesame seeds, and parsley. Remove chicken from marinade and roll in bread-crumb mixture, coating each piece well. Arrange pieces in a shallow nonstick baking dish. Brush chicken with some melted butter and bake for 40 minutes, basting with additional butter at least twice during baking.

*To toast sesame seeds: Preheat oven to 350°F (180°C, or gas mark 4) and spread sesame seeds on a baking sheet. Toast for 3 minutes, stirring once, until evenly brown. Watch carefully to avoid burning.

Prep = 15 minutes   **Chill** = 4 hours   **Cook** = 40 minutes
Yield = 2 to 4 servings

Thanksgiving Turkey with Madeira Apple Stuffing

Cheesecloth is the secret to roasting a turkey
the old-fashioned way that actually steams the meat.

- 1 fresh turkey, 18 to 22 pounds (8.2 to 10 kg)
- 1 ½ sticks (167 g) butter, softened
- Salt and pepper
- ¼ cup (60 ml) corn oil

MADEIRA APPLE STUFFING:
- 1 stick (¼ pound, or 112 g) butter
- 1 cup (100 g) chopped celery
- ½ cup (80 g) chopped onion
- 1 can (10½ ounces, or 315 ml) chicken broth
- 1 ¼ cups (295 ml) Madeira
- ½ teaspoon ground cinnamon
- 8 cups (880 g) cubed herb-seasoned stuffing mix
- 2 medium apples, cored and diced
- ½ cup (75 g) golden raisins

Preheat oven to 325°F (170°C, or gas mark 3). Remove gizzards and neck from inside the turkey. Wash turkey and pat dry. Loosely pack Madeira Apple Stuffing into turkey and close cavity with trussing skewers. Place, breast side up, in a roasting pan and rub all over with softened butter. Sprinkle with salt and pepper. Drape turkey with cheesecloth. Roast in oven for 3½ to 4 hours. Meanwhile, melt ½ stick (55 g) butter with corn oil. Every 30 minutes, remove cheesecloth from turkey and baste with butter mixture. After the first hour and a half, start basting with the turkey juices. Turkey is done when thigh juices run clear when pricked with a fork. Allow turkey to stand 30 minutes before carving.

For Madeira Apple Stuffing: In a large skillet over medium heat, melt butter and sauté celery and onion until tender. Add broth and Madeira. Bring to a boil and remove from heat. Add cinnamon, stuffing mix, apples, and raisins. Cool completely before stuffing into turkey.

Prep = 20 minutes   **Cook** = 3½ to 4½ hours
Yield = 12 to 14 servings

Tuscan Turkey Sausage and Artichoke Stew

This hearty peasant-style dish features artichokes simmered in white wine. Tomato sauce can toughen beans in a slow cooker, which is why they are added during the last hour and a half of cooking.

6 slices bacon
1 medium onion, sliced
2 cloves garlic, crushed
1 cup (125 g) baby carrots, sliced in half lengthwise
1 ¼ pounds (560 g) Italian turkey sausage, cut into 2-inch (5-cm) pieces
1 can (15 ounces, or 420 g) tomato sauce
2 teaspoons herbes de Provence
½ teaspoon ground black pepper
9 baby artichokes
2 cups (475 ml) dry white wine
2 cans (15 ounces, or 420 g, each) unsalted cannellini beans, rinsed well and drained

In a large skillet, fry bacon until crisp and drain on paper towels. Pour off fat, leaving 1 to 2 tablespoons (15 to 30 ml) in the skillet. Sauté onion, garlic, carrots, and sausage in skillet until onions are golden brown and tender. Remove with a slotted spoon, leaving excess drippings behind, and add to slow cooker. Cover with tomato sauce, herbes de Provence, and black pepper. Cook on low for 6 hours.

Meanwhile, trim outer leaves from baby artichokes, split in half, and remove fuzzy chokes. Bring wine to a boil in a large saucepan. Add artichokes, cover, and simmer for about 20 minutes, until tender. Drain well. Add beans and artichokes to the slow cooker. Crumble in the bacon. Cook for 1½ hours longer.

Prep = 20 minutes   **Cook** = 8 hours
Yield = 6 servings

Roasted Oloroso Chicken with Pine Nuts and Sherry

The glaze, crafted from the alchemy of deglazing
and reduction, is the heart of this dish from my neighbor,
Lee Steele. The pine nuts add a wholesome crunch.

1   roasting chicken (about 3 ½ pounds, or 1.6 kg)
    Salt and pepper
2   tablespoons (28 g) butter, melted
1   cup (240 ml) Oloroso sherry
1   tablespoon (8 g) cornstarch mixed with 1 tablespoon
    (15 ml) water
1   can (10 ½ ounces, or 315 ml) chicken broth
½   cup (75 g) raisins soaked in ½ cup (120 ml) Oloroso sherry
    overnight
½   cup (50 g) toasted pine nuts*

Preheat oven to 350°F (180°C, or gas mark 4). Lightly season
chicken with salt and pepper. Roast chicken for 1 hour. Combine
melted butter with 2 tablespoons (30 ml) sherry, and brush over
chicken. Bake 30 minutes longer. Remove chicken to a platter, and
pour off all but about 2 tablespoons (30 ml) fat from the pan.

Deglaze the roasting pan with remaining sherry until caramelized bits of drippings are dissolved and sherry is reduced to about
½ cup (120 ml). Add cornstarch mixture to chicken broth and
blend into reduced sherry, stirring constantly until slightly thickened. Add raisins and pine nuts and heat through. Serve chicken
quartered with glaze spooned over chicken.

*To toast pine nuts: Preheat oven to 350°F (180°C, or gas mark 4)
and spread pine nuts on a baking sheet. Toast for 6 to 8 minutes,
stirring once until golden brown. Watch carefully to avoid burning.

Prep = 10 minutes   **Cook** = 1 hour 45 minutes
Yield = 4 to 6 servings

Seafood

Cashew-Sherry Shrimp Sauté

This Asian-inspired shrimp dish makes a light lunch, appetizer, or first course. It resembles a hot salad because it's served in Boston lettuce cups.

- 1 pound (455 g) jumbo shrimp, shelled and deveined
- ¼ cup (60 ml) sherry
- 2 tablespoons (30 ml) extra-virgin olive oil
- ¼ teaspoon soy sauce
- 4 seedless mandarin oranges, peeled and sectioned
- 2 cloves garlic, minced
- ¼ cup (25 g) chopped green onions
- ¼ teaspoon red pepper flakes
- 2 tablespoons (8 g) minced fresh cilantro
- 4 large Boston lettuce leaves
- ½ cup (75 g) chopped and seeded red and yellow bell peppers
- ⅓ cup (43 g) chopped roasted cashews

In a bowl combine, shrimp, sherry, olive oil, soy sauce, oranges, garlic, green onions, red pepper flakes, and cilantro. Cover and refrigerate for 2 hours. Remove from refrigerator 30 minutes before cooking.

Heat a large skillet (or wok) over medium-high heat. Pour shrimp mixture into skillet and stir-fry until shrimp are evenly pink, about 3 minutes. Immediately divide among lettuce "cups" on plates. Sprinkle with chopped peppers and cashews for garnish.

Prep = 10 minutes   **Chill** = 2 hours plus 30 minutes standing time
Cook = 3 minutes   **Yield** = 4 servings

Almond-Crusted Shrimp

These oven-baked shrimp have been marinated
in sherry to bring out the sweet, nutty flavor of the batter.
The secret to a crispy oven-baked crust is using
Japanese panko bread crumbs.

16 raw shrimp, shelled and deveined
1 cup (240 ml) sherry
¼ cup (31 g) all-purpose flour
¼ teaspoon salt
1 egg
2 tablespoons (30 ml) water
¾ cup (38 g) panko bread crumbs
⅓ cup (30 g) sliced almonds
5 tablespoons (70 g) butter, melted

In a shallow dish, cover shrimp with sherry and cover dish with plastic wrap. Refrigerate for 2 to 3 hours.

Preheat oven to 375°F (190°C, or gas mark 5). Remove shrimp from sherry and pat dry. Combine flour and salt in a small shallow bowl. In another bowl, beat egg with water, and in a third bowl, combine bread crumbs and almonds.

Generously spray a 10 × 15-inch (25 × 37.5-cm) nonstick baking pan with nonstick spray. Coat each shrimp with flour, dip in egg wash, and then dip in crumbs. Place coated shrimp on pan and drizzle with melted butter. Bake for 30 to 35 minutes, or until shrimp are pink.

Prep = 20 minutes   **Chill** = 2 to 3 hours
Cook = 30 to 35 minutes   **Yield** = 4 servings

Asian Delight Salmon O'Brien

This grilled salmon in a spicy marinade is the inspiration of my neighbor, John O'Brien, who calls it Asian Delight. If you don't have any mirin around the house, sherry can be used in its place.

½	cup (120 ml) sesame oil
1	tablespoon (15 ml) Mongolian fire oil
2	tablespoons (30 ml) soy sauce
3	tablespoons (45 ml) mirin (sherry may also be used)
1	tablespoon (7 g) ground cumin
1	tablespoon (6 g) hot curry powder
½ to ¾	teaspoon cracked black pepper
6	salmon steaks (1¾ inches, or 4 cm)

Combine sesame oil, fire oil, soy sauce, mirin, cumin, curry powder, and pepper in a large glass or ceramic bowl. Cover with plastic and marinate salmon for 2 hours in the refrigerator, stirring once or twice. Cook over a medium hot-grill for 5 minutes on each side.

Prep = 10 minutes   **Chill** = 2 hours
Cook = 10 minutes   **Yield** = 6 servings

Dungeness Crab Cakes with Orange-Wine Sauce

This recipe differs from a typical remoulade in its orange-wine sauce. In addition, these crab cakes are pan sautéed, not deep fried.

1 egg, beaten
½ cup (115 g) mayonnaise
½ teaspoon Worcestershire sauce
1 tablespoon dried parsley
1 teaspoon Old Bay Seasoning or seafood seasoning
½ teaspoon salt
½ teaspoon black pepper
½ teaspoon mustard
6 finely crumbled saltines
1 pound (455 g) Dungeness crabmeat, picked over to remove shells
3 tablespoons (42 g) butter
3 tablespoons (45 ml) olive oil

ORANGE-WINE SAUCE:
1 cup (240 ml) orange juice
2 large shallots, minced
¼ cup (60 ml) white wine
4 tablespoons (55 g) butter, cut into pieces
2 tablespoons (28 g) plain yogurt
2 tablespoons (30 ml) cream

In mixing bowl combine egg, mayonnaise, Worcestershire sauce, parsley, and seasonings. Stir in cracker crumbs and gently fold into crabmeat.

Form mixture into 6 large or 12 small crab cakes. Chill for at least 1 hour before cooking but no longer than 24 hours. In a large, nonstick skillet over medium heat, melt butter with olive oil. Brown crab cakes for 3 to 5 minutes on each side.

For Orange-Wine Sauce: Bring orange juice to a boil and reduce by 2 tablespoons (30 ml). Add shallots, white wine, and further reduce by another 2 tablespoons (30 ml). Remove from heat and whisk in butter, yogurt, and cream.

Prep = 25 minutes **Chill** = 1 hour
Cook = 20 minutes **Yield** = 6 servings

Baked Halibut with Wine and Leeks

Leeks can be sandy, so be sure to split them in half and rinse well before slicing. Soak them in water for half an hour and let the sand settle to the bottom of the pan. Then, pat them dry on paper towels to remove excess water.

3   tablespoons (42 g) butter
1½ pounds (680 g) leeks, trimmed, washed, and sliced
1½ pounds (680 g) halibut fillets
    Salt and pepper
⅔   cup (160 ml) dry white wine
1   tablespoon (15 g) Dijon mustard

Preheat oven to 400°F (200°C, or gas mark 6). In a medium nonstick skillet, melt butter over medium heat and sauté leeks until they are soft (about 6 minutes). Line the bottom of a 2-quart (1.9-L) casserole with leeks. Arrange halibut fillets over leeks. Sprinkle lightly with salt and pepper. Blend white wine together with mustard and pour over halibut. Cover casserole and bake for 10 to 15 minutes, or until a knife meets no resistance when inserted into the thickest part of the halibut fillet.

Prep = 10 minutes   **Cook** = 16 to 21 minutes
Yield = 4 servings

Grilled Red Snapper with Mango-Lime Relish

This dish works equally well whether using red snapper or swordfish. The "heat" can be adjusted by either changing the amount of chile pepper used or stepping up to a Scotch bonnet pepper.

1 pound (455 g) red snapper or swordfish fillets, cut into 4 portions
¼ cup (60 ml) lime juice
½ cup (120 ml) white wine
2 tablespoons (4 g) snipped fresh chives
½ teaspoon minced jalapeño pepper
¼ teaspoon salt
¼ teaspoon black pepper
2 tablespoons (30 ml) olive oil

MANGO-LIME RELISH:
½ cup (160 g) apricot preserves
⅓ cup (80 ml) lime juice
1 small onion, chopped finely
1 clove garlic, crushed
¼ teaspoon allspice
¼ teaspoon salt
¼ teaspoon ground pepper
1 large ripe mango, peeled and chopped

Lightly score one side of each fish fillet and place in a shallow glass dish. Combine lime juice, wine, chives, jalapeño pepper, salt, and black pepper. Pour over fish. Cover and refrigerate for at least 1 hour or overnight. Remove fish from marinade and brush fillets on both sides with oil. Cook for 4 to 6 minutes on one side, then 3 to 5 minutes on the other, or until fish is just slightly firm to touch. Serve topped with Mango-Lime Relish.

For Mango-Lime Relish: Combine apricot preserves, lime juice, onion, garlic, allspice, salt, and pepper. Gently stir in mango, trying not to mash it up too much.

Prep = 15 minutes **Chill** = 1 hour
Cook = 7 to 11 minutes **Yield** = 4 servings

Grilled Swordfish with Red Pepper-Pecan Pesto

This swordfish presentation has a green counterpart made with green bell peppers and roasted pecans. The red version is found to be equally well received by dinner guests.

1 cup (240 ml) Riesling or other fruity white wine
1 tablespoon (15 ml) soy sauce
2 large shallots, minced
2 tablespoons (8 g) minced fresh cilantro
6 swordfish steaks (about 8 ounces, or 225 g, each)
Freshly ground pepper

ROASTED RED PEPPER PECAN PESTO:
3 red bell peppers, roasted and peeled*
½ cup (50 g) toasted pecans**
2 tablespoons (8 g) minced fresh cilantro
2 tablespoons (12 g) minced fresh ginger
2 tablespoons (20 g) minced shallots
¼ cup (25 g) grated Parmesan cheese
3 tablespoons (45 ml) extra-virgin olive oil
2 teaspoons lemon juice
Salt and red pepper flakes

Prep = 20 minutes **Chill** = 2 hours
Cook = 16 to 18 minutes **Yield** = 6 servings

In a large glass baking dish, combine wine, soy sauce, shallots, and cilantro. Add swordfish, turning to coat in marinade. Cover and refrigerate for 2 hours, turning to coat two more times. Remove from refrigerator 30 minutes before grilling.

Preheat grill to high. Brush grill grids with olive oil and grill fish on each side for 5 to 6 minutes, or until opaque throughout. Do not overcook. Season with freshly ground pepper. Serve with pesto on top of each swordfish steak.

For Roasted Red-Pepper Pecan Pesto: Combine bell peppers, nuts, cilantro, ginger, shallots, and cheese in food processor. With machine running, gradually drizzle in oil and lemon juice to make an emulsified sauce. Season with salt and red pepper flakes to taste.

*To peel peppers: Char peppers over an open flame or under a broiler until the skin blisters. Place in a plastic bag to cool. Peel off skin.

**To toast pecans: Preheat oven to 350°F (180°C, or gas mark 4) and spread pecans on a baking sheet. Toast for 6 to 8 minutes, stirring once until golden brown. Watch carefully to avoid burning.

Ceviche with Roasted Baby Corn

Traditionally a Peruvian dish, ceviche
is served as far afield as Mexico. The flesh of the
fish is not cooked but "pickled," so to speak, by the acids
of lemon and lime juices. The proteins become
denatured and the flesh sets without heat.
Wine has much the same effect.

	Juice of 4 lemons
	Juice of 4 limes
⅓	cup (80 ml) white wine
1	red onion, minced
2	tablespoons (12 g) minced fresh ginger
1	clove garlic, crushed
¼	habañero or Scotch bonnet chile pepper, minced (no seeds or ribs)
1	large celery rib, chopped
⅓	cup (21 g) minced fresh cilantro
	Salt and pepper
2	pounds (905 g) sea bass or other meaty white fish, skinned, boned, and cut into large dice
	Garlic-flavored olive oil
2	dozen fresh baby corncobs
1	pint (300 g) grape tomatoes, halved

Combine lemon and lime juice, wine, onion, ginger, garlic, chile pepper, celery, cilantro, salt, and pepper. Toss in a large glass bowl with sea bass. Cover and chill overnight. Meanwhile, rub garlic-flavored oil on a baking sheet lined with nonstick aluminum foil and arrange corncobs on foil. Preheat oven to 400°F (200°C, or gas mark 6) and roast corn in oven for 8 to 10 minutes, or until undersides of corncobs begin to brown.

Cool and chill corn in the refrigerator. Just before serving, toss sea bass with corncobs and tomatoes.

Prep = 15 minutes   **Chill** = 8 hours or overnight
Cook = 8 to 10 minutes   **Yield** = 8 servings

Country French Mussels Chardonnay

This dish is also known as Mussels Provençal.
When preparing dishes using mussels or clams,
always discard any that have failed to open their shells,
because they have gone bad.

2 tablespoons (30 ml) olive oil
4 shallots, chopped
3 cloves garlic, crushed
1 can (16 ounces, or 455 g) peeled tomatoes, drained
½ cup (30 g) fresh minced parsley
¼ teaspoon freshly cracked black pepper
½ cup (50 g) sliced ripe olives
1 cup (240 ml) Chardonnay or white wine
4 pounds (1.9 kg) fresh mussels, cleaned, with beards removed
Warm French bread

In a large (8-quart, or 7.6-L) stockpot, heat oil and add shallots and garlic.

Cook until shallots are lightly browned. Add tomatoes, breaking them up with a spoon. Add parsley, pepper, olives, and wine. Bring to a boil and cook for 4 minutes. Add mussels, tossing well to coat. Cover and cook for 3 minutes, stirring occasionally, until mussels have opened. Discard any mussels that have not opened and serve immediately in bowls with French bread.

Prep = 15 minutes **Cook** = 15 minutes **Yield** = 4 servings

Pecan-Crusted Trout Chenin Blanc

Almonds are traditionally paired with trout,
but pecans offer a hearty, crunchier texture.

4	large trout fillets
	Juice of 1 lemon
	Salt and pepper
½	cup (60 g) seasoned dry bread crumbs, divided
2	teaspoons dried rosemary
1	cup (100 g) toasted pecans*
1	egg beaten with 1 tablespoon (15 ml) water
⅓	cup (42 g) all-purpose flour
2	tablespoons (28 g) butter
2	tablespoons (30 ml) vegetable oil
1	cup (240 ml) Chenin Blanc

Coat trout fillets with lemon juice and sprinkle lightly with salt and pepper. Allow to stand for about 10 minutes. Combine ¼ cup (30 g) bread crumbs with rosemary and pecans and coarsely grind in food processor. Combine with remaining bread crumbs in a shallow dish. Put egg wash in a shallow bowl. Dredge trout fillets with flour and dip in egg wash. Place, skin side up, in pecan crumb mixture, pressing pecan mixture into flesh.

In large nonstick skillet, melt 1 tablespoon each of butter (14 g) and oil (15 ml). Place fillets skin-side up, two at a time, with coating facing down. Cook until golden brown, for 3 to 4 minutes. Using spatula, carefully turn fillets skin side down. Cook for 3 minutes, until opaque. Transfer trout to a warm platter and repeat with remaining two fillets, oil, and butter. Deglaze pan with Chenin Blanc wine and reduce until syrupy. Drizzle over trout fillets.

*To toast pecans: Preheat oven to 350°F (180°C, or gas mark 4) and spread pecans on a baking sheet. Bake for 6 to 8 minutes, stirring once or twice, until evenly golden brown. Watch carefully to avoid burning.

Prep = 20 minutes   **Cook** = 12 to 16 minutes   **Yield** = 4 servings

Mediterranean Tilapia

Tilapia is an African freshwater fish that has far-reaching popularity in many cuisines. Its mild flavor adapts to many recipes. This Mediterranean-inspired version is extremely heart healthy, with olive oil, garlic, and tomatoes.

2	tablespoons (30 ml) olive oil
1	clove garlic, minced
½	cup (80 g) chopped onion
1	can (14 ounces, or 400 g) Italian stewed tomatoes
¼	cup (25 g) sliced, pitted green olives
¼	cup (25 g) sliced, pitted black olives
½	lemon
¼	cup (60 ml) dry white wine
¼	teaspoon black pepper
6	tilapia fillets
	Saffron rice

Heat oil in a large nonstick skillet over medium-high heat. Add garlic and onion and sauté for about 5 minutes. Add tomatoes, olives, lemon half, wine, and black pepper. Simmer for 10 minutes. Add tilapia fillets to sauce and simmer for 10 more minutes, or until fish flakes easily. Remove lemon half and serve tilapia over rice, spooning sauce over tilapia.

Prep = 15 minutes   **Cook** = 25 to 30 minutes   **Yield** = 6 servings

Mirin-Glazed Salmon with Honey, Soy Sauce, and Wasabi

Japanese sweet rice wine makes mirin-marinated salmon such a popular dish on Asian fusion-style restaurant menus that it's now very mainstream. It can be prepared under the broiler or grilled.

½ cup (120 ml) mirin
2 tablespoons (30 ml) soy sauce
¼ cup (60 ml) rice vinegar (unseasoned)
1 tablespoon (6 g) finely grated peeled fresh ginger
4 pieces (6 ounces, or 170 g, each) salmon fillet

FOR SAUCES:
2 tablespoons (30 ml) soy sauce
¼ cup (85 g) honey
1 tablespoon (15 ml) fresh lime juice
2 teaspoons wasabi powder
1 tablespoon (15 ml) water

Lime wedges

Stir together mirin, soy sauce, rice vinegar, and ginger in a shallow dish. Add fish, skin side up, and marinate. Cover with plastic wrap and let stand at room temperature for 10 minutes. Preheat broiler or grill. Broil salmon, skin side down, on an oiled rack of broiler pan, 5 to 7 inches (12.5 to 17.5 cm) from heat, until fish is cooked through (about 6 minutes). The same time applies if cooked on an oiled grill.

Meanwhile, boil soy sauce, honey, and lime juice in a small saucepan until thickened (about 4 minutes). Stir together wasabi powder and water. Drizzle soy-honey glaze over salmon and serve with a puddle of wasabi sauce next to each fillet on the plate. Garnish with lime wedges.

Prep = 20 minutes   **Cook** = 20 minutes   **Yield** = 4 servings

Spanish Paella

Traditionally, Spanish Paella is a mélange of seafood, chicken, and rice. The shrimp, squid, clams, and mussels outvote the chicken to make this much more a seafood dish than a poultry dish. Pricey saffron is essential to this dish. Fortunately, it takes only a few threads of this culinary "gold" to make the dish.

1	tablespoon (15 ml) olive oil
5	bacon slices, chopped
1	broiler/fryer chicken (about 3 pounds, or 1.4 kg), cut up
	Salt and pepper
2	cups (320 g) chopped onions
4	cloves garlic, crushed
2	cups (370 g) uncooked long-grain white rice
1	jar (7 ounces, or 200 g) roasted, sliced pimientos with juice
½	teaspoon crushed saffron threads
2	cups (475 ml) chicken broth
1	cup (240 ml) dry white wine
½	cup (120 ml) clam juice
1	pound (455 g) large, uncooked shrimp, peeled and deveined
1	pound (455 g) clean squid, bodies cut into ½-inch (1.3-cm) rings
1	dozen clams, scrubbed
1	dozen mussels, debearded
1	cup (130 g) frozen peas, thawed
	Lemon wedges

Prep = 20 minutes   **Cook** = 1 hour, 15 minutes
Yield = 6 to 8 servings

Preheat oven to 450°F (230°C, or gas mark 8). Heat olive oil in a large stockpot over medium-high heat. Add chopped bacon and cook until fat is rendered, about 6 minutes. Using slotted spoon, transfer bacon to paper towels and drain. Set aside. Sprinkle chicken pieces with salt and pepper. Add chicken to bacon drippings in pot and cook over medium heat until browned (about 7 minutes per side). Using tongs, remove chicken from pot.

Add chopped onions and garlic to the pot and sauté until beginning to brown, scraping up any browned bits. Stir in rice, roasted pimientos with juices, and saffron. Add chicken broth, white wine, and clam juice to the pot and bring mixture to a simmer. Remove from heat. Pour rice mixture into a large glass or ceramic casserole. Arrange chicken, shrimp, squid, clams, and mussels in rice mixture. Sprinkle with chopped bacon and peas. Cover with foil.

Bake paella until chicken is cooked through, clams and mussels open, and rice is tender, about 45 minutes. Be sure to discard any clams or mussels that do not open. Remove foil from baking dish. Let paella stand 10 minutes and serve with lemon wedges.

Sweet and Savory Glazed Salmon

As with Japanese-style mirin-glazed salmon,
sweet and salty flavors work well with this dish. This is
such an easy dish to prepare that it should be kept in mind
when time is short for dinner or for guests.

¾   cup (175 ml) dry white wine
4   tablespoons (55 g) butter, cut into tablespoons
1   teaspoon Old Bay Seasoning
1   skinless salmon fillet (about 2 pounds, or 905 g)
    Salt and pepper
⅓   cup (80 g) spicy brown mustard
⅓   cup (75 g) firmly packed light brown sugar
⅓   cup (90 g) sliced almonds

Preheat oven to 350°F (180°C, or gas mark 4). Boil wine, butter, and Old Bay Seasoning in a small saucepan for 3 minutes. Sprinkle salmon on both sides with salt and pepper. Place fish on a jelly roll or sheet cake pan and pour wine mixture over the top. Bake until fish is opaque in the center (about 14 minutes). Remove from oven. Combine mustard and brown sugar. Spread over salmon.

Preheat broiler, spread almonds over salmon, and broil for 3 minutes, or until sugar is caramelized and almonds are toasted.

Prep = 10 minutes   **Cook** = 14 minutes   **Yield** = 4 to 6 servings

Soft-Shell Crabs Vermouth

The addition of vermouth to the soft-shell
crabs amandine gives the dish an interesting character.
If serving as an entrée, consider allowing
two per person.

- 1 stick (¼ pound, or 112 g) butter
- ⅓ cup (30 g) sliced, blanched almonds
- 4 small soft-shell crabs, dressed
  All-purpose flour, for dredging
- 1 tablespoon (15 ml) lemon juice
- ¼ cup vermouth
- 1 tablespoon (4 g) minced fresh parsley
- 1 tablespoon (4 g) chives
  Lemon wedges

Melt 1 tablespoon (14 g) butter in a small skillet and sauté
almonds, stirring constantly until golden brown. Meanwhile,
dredge crabs lightly in flour and shake off excess. Heat remaining
butter in a medium nonstick skillet. Once the butter is hot and
foaming, add crabs. Sauté over high heat, turning occasionally
with tongs, until crisp and reddish brown, about 5 minutes.
Transfer crabs to a heated platter. Add lemon juice and vermouth
to the skillet and bring juices to a boil. Stir in parsley and chives,
then pour over crabs. Top with almonds. Serve with lemon
wedges.

Prep = 10 minutes **Cook** = 10 minutes **Yield** = 2 servings

Sole Amandine

Nothing could be more timeless than this classic
preparation for fillet of sole. Flounder works just as well.
Sometimes it's hard to cook all six fillets at once in
one skillet. If so, divide the butter and oil in
half and sauté three at a time.

- 6   tablespoons (84 g) butter
- 1   tablespoon (15 ml) olive oil
- 6   Dover or lemon sole fillets
    All-purpose flour, for dredging
- 2   eggs, beaten
- ½   cup (45 g) sliced almonds
- ⅓   cup (80 ml) white wine
- 2   tablespoons (30 ml) fresh lemon juice
    Lemon wedges

Melt 5 tablespoons (70 g) butter with oil in a very large nonstick
skillet. Dip sole fillets in flour and then in egg. Sauté fillets until
golden (about 2 or 3 minutes on each side). Remove from skillet
and transfer to a warm platter.

Melt the remaining 1 tablespoon (14 g) of butter, scraping pan,
add almonds, and sauté until lightly golden. Add wine and lemon
juice and simmer until thickened. Pour over fillets and serve with
lemon wedges.

Prep = 10 minutes   **Cook** = 14 to 16 minutes   **Yield** = 6 servings

Baja Fish Tacos

A splash of wine can be added to even the
humblest of dishes—like fish tacos—to make them
more flavorful and adventurous.

   1   package (1.25 ounces, or (35 g) taco seasoning mix
   ½   cup (115 g) cup sour cream
   ½   cup (115 g) mayonnaise
   ¼   cup (15 g) minced fresh cilantro
   1   pound (455 g) cod fillets, cut into 1-inch (2.5 cm) cubes
   ½   cup (120 ml) white wine
   3   tablespoons (45 ml) extra-virgin olive oil

  12   taco shells
       Shredded romaine lettuce and diced tomatoes

Combine half of taco seasoning mix with sour cream, mayonnaise,
and cilantro and chill. Marinate cod, in white wine, refrigerating,
covered, for at least 1 to 2 hours. Drain. Toss cod with oil and
remaining seasoning mix.

Transfer cod mixture to a medium non-stick skillet. Cook, stirring
constantly, over medium-high heat, until fish flakes easily with
a fork, about 4 to 5 minutes. Fill taco shells with fish. Top with
lettuce, tomatoes, and seasoned sour cream mixture.

Prep = 20 minutes   **Chill** = 1 to 2 hours   **Cook** = 5 minutes
Yield = 6 servings

Pasta

Gorgonzola Linguine with Walnuts and White Zinfandel

It's important to toss the pasta with the sauce at the last minute because the pasta tends to absorb the sauce if reheated. A half portion of this serves as an appetizer just as well as a full portion as an entrée.

- ¾ cup (175 ml) light cream
- ½ cup (120 ml) heavy cream
- ¾ cup (175 ml) White Zinfandel
- 8 ounces (225 g) Gorgonzola cheese, crumbled
- ¾ cup (90 g) chopped walnuts, toasted*
- ½ teaspoon minced fresh rosemary
- 1 pound (455 g) dried linguine

In a medium saucepan, heat the creams and wine over medium heat. Add Gorgonzola and simmer until melted. Stir in ½ cup (60 g) walnuts and rosemary.

In large pot of boiling, salted water, cook linguine until al dente. Drain and transfer to a warmed serving bowl. Spoon cheese sauce over the top and sprinkle with remaining walnuts.

*For toasted walnuts: Preheat oven to 350°F (180°C, or gas mark 4) and spread walnuts on a baking sheet. Toast for 6 to 8 minutes, turning once, until golden brown. Watch carefully to avoid burning.

Prep = 20 minutes **Cook** = 20 minutes **Yield** = 4 servings

Cincinnati Chili Spaghetti with Chianti

Chili over spaghetti is a phenomenon not limited to Cincinnati, Ohio. This dish is also a regular item in diners and home-style restaurants across the Midwest. Adding Chianti gives the dish a whole new dimension.

1 ½ pounds (680 g) lean ground beef
1 medium onion, chopped
½ cup (75 g) chopped and seeded green bell pepper
2 cloves garlic, crushed
1 can (28 ounces, or 785 g) diced tomatoes, undrained
1 can (19 ounces, or 532 g) red kidney beans, drained
1 can (8 ounces, or 225 g) tomato sauce
⅔ cup (160 ml) Chianti
1 tablespoon (8 g) chili powder
1 teaspoon salt
1 teaspoon Worcestershire sauce
1 package (7 ounces, or 200 g) spaghetti

In a large nonstick skillet over medium heat, cook beef, onion, bell pepper, and garlic, stirring occasionally, until beef is browned and onion and pepper are tender. Drain off excess fat. Stir in tomatoes, beans, tomato sauce, Chianti, chili powder, salt, and Worcestershire sauce. Bring to a boil and then reduce to a simmer. Cook for at least 15 minutes, or until sauce is the thickness you prefer.

Meanwhile, cook spaghetti in a large pot of boiling salted water until al dente. Drain well. Serve spaghetti in individual bowls with sauce over top.

Prep = 15 minutes   **Cook** = 30 to 40 minutes   **Yield** = 6 servings

Fresh Tomato Penne Pinot Noir

With only 1 tablespoon (15 ml) of olive oil,
this is a suitable dish for anyone on a low-fat diet.

8 ounces (225 g) dried whole-wheat penne pasta
1 tablespoon (15 ml) extra-virgin olive oil
2 cloves garlic, crushed
1 shallot, minced
12 medium roma (plum) tomatoes, chopped coarsely
¼ cup (60 ml) Pinot Noir or red wine
2 tablespoons (8 g) chopped fresh basil
  Salt and pepper

In a large pot of boiling, salted water, cook penne until al dente. Drain well and turn into a warm serving bowl.

Heat olive oil in a medium nonstick skillet and sauté garlic and shallot for about a minute over medium-high heat, stirring frequently. Add tomatoes and wine. Cook, stirring frequently, for about 8 minutes, or until sauce is slightly thickened. Stir in basil and season with salt and pepper to taste. Spoon sauce over penne.

Prep = 15 minutes **Cook** = 15 to 20 minutes **Yield** = 4 servings

Spaghetti Bolognese
with Roasted Zucchini

The secret ingredient
to a certain Long Island restaurant's Bolognese sauce?
Cream. Zucchini can be roasted right in the oven,
even the toaster oven.

- ¼ cup (60 ml) extra-virgin olive oil
- 4 ounces (115 g) pancetta, minced
- 1 onion, chopped finely
- 1 carrot, peeled and chopped finely
- 1 celery stalk, chopped finely
- 8 ounces (225 g) lean ground veal
- 4 ounces (115 g) lean ground pork
- ⅔ cup (160 ml) dry white wine
- 1 cup (240 ml) beef broth
- 1 can (12 ounces, or 340 g) peeled whole tomatoes, chopped coarsely, liquid reserved
- ⅓ cup (80 ml) heavy cream
- ⅓ cup (33 g) grated Parmesan cheese
  Salt and pepper
- 1 pound (455 g) fresh spaghetti
- 1 roasted zucchini*

Heat olive oil in a large, heavy-duty saucepan over medium-high heat. Add pancetta, onion, carrot, and celery, and sauté for 6 to 8 minutes, or until golden.

Add ground veal and pork to vegetable mixture and sauté until browned. Add wine and stir to scrape up the browned bits from the bottom of the pan. Continue cooking until liquid is reduced to half.

Add beef broth, tomatoes, and reserved tomato liquid. Reduce heat to simmer and cook, stirring frequently, for 35 to 40 minutes or until thickened. Stir in cream and Parmesan cheese. Heat through for another 3 to 5 minutes. Season to taste with salt and pepper.

In a large pot of boiling, salted water, cook spaghetti until al dente. Drain well and turn into a warm serving bowl. Toss with sauce. Add zucchini and gently toss so it doesn't break up too much.

*To roast zucchini: Preheat oven to 425°F (220°C, or gas mark 7). Lightly brush nonstick aluminum foil with a coating of garlic-infused oil. Slice zucchini on the diagonal and arrange on foil. Bake for 6 to 8 minutes on the bottom rack of oven until the undersides of slices begin to brown.

Prep = 20 minutes   **Cook** = 1¼ hours   **Yield** = 6 servings

Orzo with Sausage and Cranberries

This makes a nice side dish to
holiday meals featuring roast turkey or duckling. *Orzo*
means "barley" in Latin, but it's actually a rice-shaped pasta
made out of hard wheat semolina, and it's
smaller than a pine nut.

3	slices bacon, cut into small strips
8	ounces (225 g) breakfast sausage links, sliced
3	shallots, minced
½	cup (50 g) sliced scallions
12	ounces (340 g) orzo
2 ½	cups (570 ml) chicken broth
1	cup (240 ml) Marsala wine
1½	cups (355 ml) orange juice
½	cup (60 g) dried cranberries
½	teaspoon dried sage

In a large nonstick skillet, brown bacon until crisp and set aside.
Add sausages to the pan and brown in bacon drippings. Set
sausage aside with the bacon. Add shallots and scallions to drippings in the pan and sauté until tender. Stir in orzo, chicken broth,
Marsala, orange juice, cranberries, and sage. Bring to a boil, stirring occasionally. Reduce heat and simmer, covered, until most of
the liquid is absorbed (about 15 minutes). Remove from heat and
let stand, covered, for 10 minutes. Toss and serve.

Prep = 15 minutes **Cook** = 40 minutes **Yield** = 8 servings

Penne with Wild Mushrooms in Marsala

The combination of fresh and dried
mushrooms gives this sauce a lot of woodsy depth.

- 2 large shallots, sliced
- 1 clove garlic, crushed
- 2 tablespoons (30 ml) extra-virgin olive oil
- 8 ounces (225 g) mixed fresh wild mushrooms (porcinis, shiitakes, and/or chanterelles), sliced
- 2 ounces (55 g) dried porcini mushrooms, soaked for 20 minutes in warm water
- ½ cup (120 ml) Marsala
- 2 cups (475 ml) chicken stock
- 1 pound (455 g) boneless, skinless chicken breast, cut into julienne strips
- 1 teaspoon minced fresh thyme
- 1 tablespoon (4 g) minced fresh flat-leaf parsley
- Salt and freshly ground pepper
- 1 pound (455 g) dried whole-wheat penne

In a medium nonstick skillet, sauté shallots and garlic in olive oil until soft but not brown, 2 to 3 minutes. Add the sliced mushrooms. Drain dried porcini mushrooms, reserving the soaking liquid. Chop the drained mushrooms and add to skillet. Sauté for about 10 minutes, until mushrooms have softened and liquid has evaporated.

Add Marsala and stir to scrape the bottom of the pan. Boil down liquid, reducing until somewhat thickened. Add chicken stock and reserved mushroom-soaking liquid, chicken, thyme, and parsley. Bring to a boil and reduce heat. Simmer for about 20 minutes, or until chicken is opaque and sauce is slightly thickened. Season to taste with salt and pepper and keep warm.

In a large pot of boiling salted water, cook pasta until al dente. Drain and toss with mushroom sauce.

Prep = 20 minutes   **Cook** = 40 to 45 minutes   **Yield** = 4 servings

Salmon and Asparagus Penne

Penne tossed with asparagus and salmon is a
perfect spring dish. The sauce is lightly thickened
to give it body without using heavy cream.

1	package (16 ounces, or 455 g) dried spinach-flavored penne
2	dozen asparagus spears
1	red bell pepper
1	green bell pepper
2	skinless salmon fillets (6 ounces, or 170 g, each)
4	tablespoons (55 g) butter
2	cloves garlic, crushed
1	cup (240 ml) white wine
	Juice and zest of 1 lemon
1	tablespoon (4 g) minced fresh dill
1	tablespoon (4 g) minced fresh parsley
1 ½	tablespoons (12 g) cornstarch mixed with 1½ tablespoons (25 ml) water
1	cup (240 ml) chicken broth
1	cup (240 ml) half-and-half

In a large pot of boiling water, cook penne until al dente. Drain and transfer to a warm serving bowl.

Cut asparagus into 2-inch (5-cm) pieces. Split bell peppers in half, remove seeds, and slice into 1-inch (2.5-cm) pieces. Cut salmon into 2-inch (5-cm) cubes.

In a large skillet over medium-high heat, melt 2 tablespoons (28 g) butter and sauté peppers and asparagus for 2 minutes. Add salmon, cover, reduce heat, and continue cooking for 5 minutes.

In a medium saucepan, cook garlic in remaining butter for about 1 minute. Add wine, lemon juice and zest, dill, and parsley, and bring to a boil. Stir cornstarch mixture into broth. Add to saucepan along with half-and-half and cook, stirring constantly, until mixture thickens. Stir sauce into salmon mixture in skillet. Pour over pasta and toss.

Prep = 15 minutes **Cook** = 20 minutes
Yield = 6 servings

Penne with Pork and Artichokes in Rosemary Wine Sauce

This Tuscany-inspired recipe makes a robust and hearty stewlike sauce. To achieve even more of a Mediterranean flavor, substitute lamb for pork.

6	baby artichokes
1	lemon, halved and seeded
	Olive oil, for sautéing
1	pound (455 g) pork shoulder, cut into 1-inch (2.5-cm) cubes
1	small onion, sliced thinly
1 ½	cups (355 ml) dry white wine
1 ½	cups (355 ml) chicken stock
	Salt and pepper
1	can (12 ounces, or 340 g) peeled whole tomatoes
1	tablespoon (4 g) minced fresh flat-leaf parsley
3	sprigs fresh rosemary
½	cup (50 g) sliced pitted black olives
1	pound (455 g) regular or sun-dried tomato penne pasta

Trim thick outer leaves, stems, and tops of artichokes. Rub all cut surfaces with lemon. Squeeze lemon juice into a bowl of water and add artichokes. In a medium nonstick skillet, heat olive oil over medium-high heat and sauté pork and onion until pork is browned (8 to 10 minutes). Add wine and chicken stock, stirring to scrape up the browned bits from the bottom of the pan. Increase the heat to high and cook to reduce liquid by half. Season broth with salt and pepper to taste.

Add tomatoes (with liquid) and return to boil. Add artichokes, parsley, and rosemary. Reduce to a simmer. Cover and cook until artichokes are tender (45 to 50 minutes). Stir in olives and season with salt and pepper to taste. Remove rosemary sprigs. Set aside and keep warm.

In a large pot of boiling water, cook the penne until al dente. Drain well and transfer to a warm serving dish. Toss with pork sauce and serve.

Prep = 20 minutes   **Cook** = 1 hour, 20 minutes
Yield = 6 servings

Fettuccini with Spinach, Creamy Goat Cheese Sauce, and Pine Nuts

Goat cheese, pine nuts, and spinach work
well together, whether they're on a salad or a pasta
dish. The goat cheese tends to be lumpy, so press the sauce
through a sieve first and keep it warm in a double boiler.
The combination is also great with tortellini.

³⁄₄ cup (175 ml) dry white wine
3 cloves garlic (do not crush)
½ teaspoon sea salt
2 cups (475 ml) heavy cream
5 ounces (140 g) aged, creamy goat cheese
1 pound (455 g) fettuccine
½ cup (70 g) pine nuts
1 teaspoon (5 ml) extra-virgin olive oil
2 cups (60 g) fresh baby spinach

In a medium saucepan, combine wine, garlic, and salt and bring to a boil over medium-high heat. Cook for about 5 minutes, or until reduced to ¼ cup (60 ml). Discard garlic. Stir in cream and goat cheese with a wire whisk until cheese has melted. Press sauce through a sieve and keep warm in a double boiler.

Meanwhile, cook pasta in a large pot of boiling, salted water until al dente; drain well. In a small saucepan, sauté pine nuts in olive oil until golden brown. Add spinach to pan and stir just until wilted. Turn into a warmed serving bowl and toss with sauce and spinach fettuccine. Serve at once.

Prep = 20 minutes   **Cook** = 20 minutes   **Yield** = 4 servings

Seafood and Sun-Dried Tomato Linguini Soave

*Soave can be neutral, fruity, or nutty
flavored, depending on the wine's producer.
Any type makes an excellent "broth"
for simmering shrimp and clams.*

1	pound (455 g) fresh or dried sun-dried tomato linguini
¼	cup (60 ml) extra-virgin olive oil
3	shallots, minced
3	cloves garlic, crushed
1	cup (110 g) oil-packed sun-dried tomatoes, drained and chopped
1 ½	cups (355 ml) Soave or other white wine
1	pound (455 g) large shrimp, peeled and deveined
2	pounds (905 g) littleneck clams, scrubbed
1	teaspoon salt
½	teaspoon freshly ground black pepper
2	cups (60 g) baby romaine lettuce

In a large pot of boiling, salted water, cook linguini until al dente. Drain well and keep warm in a bowl while preparing sauce.

Heat olive oil in a large, heavy skillet over medium heat. Add shallots and garlic and cook for 3 minutes, until tender but not brown. Add sun-dried tomatoes and cook for another minute. Add wine, shrimp, and clams and bring liquid to a boil. Reduce heat, cover, and simmer until shrimp are pink and clams have opened (about 7 minutes). Discard any clams that have not opened.

Add linguini to the skillet. Season with salt and pepper. Toss in baby romaine. Mound pasta on a large serving platter and serve immediately.

Prep = 25 minutes   **Cook** = 20 minutes   **Yield** = 6 servings

Sesame Chicken and Asparagus in Peanut Sauce

Soba is the Japanese word for "buckwheat," and soba noodles are made from buckwheat flour. Linguine can also be used.

8 to 9	ounces (225 to 255 g) soba or buckwheat noodles
2	cloves garlic, crushed
1	tablespoon (8 g) candied ginger
¼	cup (60 g) brown sugar
1	tablespoon (15 ml) red wine vinegar
1	tablespoon (16 g) chunky peanut butter
3	tablespoons (45 ml) soy sauce
3	tablespoons (45 ml) mirin
6	tablespoons (90 ml) sesame oil
1	tablespoon (15 ml) hot chile oil
2	cups (280 g) sliced cooked chicken
⅓	cup (48 g) toasted sesame seeds, divided*
1	pound (455 g) pencil-thin asparagus, trimmed
4	scallions cut into 2-inch (5-cm) julienne pieces
	Small cucumber, halved, seeded, and cut into ¼-inch (6-mm) dice

Cook noodles according to package directions. Combine garlic, ginger, brown sugar, vinegar, peanut butter, soy sauce, and mirin in food processor until smooth. With processor running, drizzle in sesame and chile oil. Toss chicken with sauce and 4 tablespoons of the sesame seeds. Slice asparagus into 1-inch (2.5-cm) lengths. Blanch in boiling water for 1 minute. Drain in a colander and rinse with cold water. Place soba noodles and chicken in the bottom of a large, flat serving bowl. Layer asparagus on top and sprinkle with scallions, cucumber, and remaining sesame seeds. Serve at room temperature.

*To toast sesame seeds: Preheat oven to 350°F (180°C, or gas mark 4) and spread sesame seeds on a baking sheet. Toast for 3 minutes, stirring once, until evenly brown. Watch carefully to avoid burning.

Prep = 20 minutes   **Cook** = 5 to 7 minutes   **Yield** = 6 servings

Tuscan-Style Chicken Tetrazzini

Rumor has it that chicken Tetrazzini
was invented at the turn of the century in Charleston,
South Carolina, for the soprano Luisa Tetrazzini.

6   tablespoons (84 g) butter, cut in tablespoons
4   ounces (115 g) fresh mushrooms, sliced
1   clove garlic, crushed
¼   cup (31 g) all-purpose flour
1   teaspoon salt
¼   teaspoon black pepper
½   cup (120 ml) chicken broth
½   cup (120 ml) Pinot Grigio or white wine
1   cup (240 ml) half-and-half
¾   cup (175 ml) heavy cream beaten with 3 egg yolks
1   cup (100 g) grated Parmesan cheese
3   cups (420 g) cubed cooked chicken
½   cup (50 g) drained, sliced ripe olives
½   cup (55 g) sun-dried tomatoes, chopped
7   ounces (200 g) spaghetti, cooked according
    to package directions until al dente, and drained

In a small skillet, melt 2 tablespoons (28 g) butter over medium
heat and sauté mushrooms and garlic for about 5 minutes, or
until mushrooms are tender. Set aside. In a large saucepan, melt
remaining butter and blend in flour, salt, and pepper. Cook, stirring
constantly, until mixture bubbles. Blend in chicken broth, wine,
half-and-half, and cream mixed with egg yolks. Cook, stirring constantly, until sauce thickens and bubbles. Stir in ⅔ cup (66 g)
Parmesan cheese. Combine chicken, olives, tomatoes, and
spaghetti in a large, buttered casserole dish. Pour sauce over the
top and sprinkle with remaining cheese. Preheat oven to 350°F
(180°C, or gas mark 4). Bake casserole for 25 to 30 minutes, or
until cheese topping is golden brown.

Prep = 20 minutes   **Cook** = 45 to 50 minutes   **Yield** = 6 servings

Spaghetti Carbonara

Spaghetti Carbonara has traditionally been prepared tableside in a chafing dish at favorite Italian restaurants. A dash of Pinot Grigio added to the original version puts an interesting spin on a classic.

- 2 tablespoons (30 ml) extra-virgin olive oil
- 1 onion, chopped
- 4 ounces (115 g) pancetta, diced
- 3 tablespoons (45 ml) Pinot Grigio or other white wine
- 4 egg yolks
- ½ cup (120 ml) heavy cream
- 1 cup (100 g) freshly grated Parmesan cheese
  Salt and black pepper
- 1 pound (455 g) dried spaghetti
- 2 tablespoons (8 g) minced Italian flat-leaf parsley

Heat olive oil in a small skillet over medium heat and sauté onion until tender (about 3 minutes). Add pancetta and cook until lightly browned. Add wine and simmer until most of the liquid has evaporated. Remove from heat and allow to cool slightly.

Beat egg yolks in a bowl with heavy cream and Parmesan cheese and blend into onion mixture. Season with salt and pepper to taste.

In a large pot of boiling water, cook spaghetti until al dente. Drain well and turn into a large warm bowl. Toss with carbonara sauce mixture until well coated. Serve on individual plates garnished with chopped parsley.

Prep = 15 minutes **Cook** = 15 to 20 minutes
Yield = 6 servings

Mom's Mac & Cheese

The original version of this macaroni and cheese
recipe was made with Gouda and Jarlsberg cheeses.
The addition of bacon and wine give it a European flavor,
like a macaroni quiche Lorraine.

- 7   ounces (200 g) uncooked elbow macaroni
- 6   tablespoons (84 g) butter
- ¼   cup (40 g) minced onion
- 6   tablespoons (48 g) all-purpose flour
- ½   teaspoon salt
- ¼   teaspoon pepper
- 2   cups (475 ml) milk
- ½   cup (120 ml) half-and-half
- ½   cup (120 ml) Riesling or other white wine
- 1   cup (120 g) grated Gouda cheese
- 1   cup (120 g) grated Jarlsberg cheese
- ⅓   cup (27 g) crumbled crisp-cooked bacon

In a large pot of boiling salted water, cook macaroni according to
package directions and drain. Preheat oven to 350°F (180°C, or
gas mark 4). Melt butter in a large saucepan over medium heat.
Add onion and sauté, stirring frequently, until soft, but do not
allow to brown. Blend in flour, salt, and pepper to make a bubbling
roux and blend in milk, half-and-half, and wine. Cook, stirring
constantly, until mixture thickens and comes to a boil. Add cheeses
and blend until melted. Stir in bacon. Pour into an ungreased,
2-quart (1.9-L) casserole and bake for 20 to 25 minutes, until
bubbling.

Prep = 15 minutes **Cook** = 30 to 35 minutes
Yield = 4 servings

Lisa's All-Purpose Alfredo Sauce with Pinot Grigio

Lisa O'Brien, my neighbor and
chief recipe taster, makes this ultra-rich Alfredo sauce
in a large batch. There's enough to toss with 2 pounds (905 g)
of pasta. You can also keep it in a jar to use a little at a time,
because it's just as good on fettuccini as it is on tortellini.
Simply reheat and use as much as needed. In the
mood for variety? Toss in peas, pancetta,
even porcini mushrooms.

- 1   stick (¼ pound, or 112 g) butter
- 2   shallots, minced
- 2   cloves garlic, crushed
- ⅓   cup (80 ml) Pinot Grigio or other white wine
- 2   cups (475 ml) heavy cream
- 1   cup (100 g) freshly grated Parmesan cheese
-     Salt and pepper
- 2   pounds (905 g) pasta of your choice
-     Optional: diced pancetta, peas, and/or sautéed porcini mushrooms

Melt 2 tablespoons (28 g) butter in a medium saucepan and sauté shallots and garlic until soft (do not allow to brown). Add wine and reduce liquid by half. Add remaining butter and stir until melted. Blend in cream and cheese and reduce to low. Simmer until just slightly thickened. Season to taste with salt and pepper.

In a large pot of boiling salted water, cook pasta until al dente. Drain and transfer to a warm serving bowl. Toss with sauce. If desired, you can add pancetta, peas, and/or mushrooms.

Prep = 10 minutes   **Cook** = 15 to 20 minutes
Yield = 8 to 10 servings

Side Dishes

Green Beans with Shiitake Mushrooms

This side accents any Asian-inspired dish.
Haricots verts are very thin and deep green in color,
and loosely translate to French green beans. Adding a
touch of baking soda preserves the beautiful color
during the cooking process.

1   quart (945 ml) water
¼   teaspoon baking soda
1 ½   pounds (680 g) haricots verts, or French green beans
⅓   cup (37 g) slivered almonds
8   ounces (225 g) fresh shiitake mushrooms
1   tablespoon (15 ml) olive oil
1   tablespoon (15 ml) sesame oil
2   tablespoons (30 ml) mirin
1   tablespoon (15 ml) soy sauce

In a large saucepan, bring 1 quart (945 ml) water to a boil with baking soda. Trim haricots verts and add to boiling water. Cook for 6 to 8 minutes, or until tender-crisp. Immediately rinse under cold water to stop cooking, and let drain.

Meanwhile, in a small but heavy nonstick skillet, stir-fry almonds until they turn a toasty golden brown (no oil is necessary) and set aside.

Remove tough stems from shiitake mushrooms and slice. In a medium skillet over medium heat, add oils and sauté mushrooms for 3 minutes, add mirin and soy sauce, and continue cooking for 3 more minutes. Gently stir in beans to heat through and toss with almonds.

Prep = 10 minutes   **Cook** = 20 minutes   **Yield** = 6 servings

Au Gratin Potatoes with White Wine and White Cheddar Cheese

For years, classic au gratin potatoes have
been made with sharp Cheddar cheese. In breaking
with convention, white Cheddar is used in this au gratin.
Add white wine and a new spin has been placed on
an all-time favorite.

¼ cup (40 g) chopped onion
3 tablespoons (42 g) butter
2 tablespoons (16 g) all-purpose flour
½ teaspoon salt
¼ teaspoon pepper
1 ¼ cups (295 ml) half-and-half
1 ¼ cups (295 ml) dry white wine
2 cups (240 g) grated white Cheddar cheese
6 medium potatoes, sliced wafer thin
¼ cup (30 g) dry bread crumbs

Preheat oven to 375°F (190°C, or gas mark 5). Spray a 1½-quart
(1.4-L) casserole with nonstick cooking spray. In a 2-quart (1.9-L)
saucepan over medium heat, sauté onion in butter until tender,
stirring occasionally (about 2 minutes). Blend in flour, salt, and
pepper. Cook, stirring constantly, until bubbling; remove from heat.
  Blend in half-and-half and wine. Heat, stirring constantly with a
wire whisk, until mixture comes to a boil. Boil for 1 minute and stir
in 1½ cups (180 g) of cheese until melted. Spread potatoes in
casserole. Pour cheese sauce over potatoes. Bake, uncovered,
for 1 hour. In a small bowl, mix bread crumbs with remaining
½ cup (60 g) cheese. Sprinkle over potatoes and bake for 15
minutes longer, or until topping is browned and bubbling.

Prep = 15 minutes   **Cook** = 1 hour, 25 minutes   **Yield** = 6 servings

---

Broccolini
with Pine Nuts

Broccolini resembles broccoli rabe, only it's
not as bitter. For that reason, it can be used in recipes
as a complement to asparagus. The flavor is often
described as a cross between asparagus and broccoli.

½ cup (68 g) pine nuts
1 tablespoon (15 ml) olive oil
1 tablespoon (14 g) butter
2 pounds (905 g) broccolini, trimmed
½ cup (120 ml) dry white wine
   Salt and pepper

In a large nonstick skillet over medium heat, sauté pine nuts in
olive oil and butter until they just begin to turn golden brown.
Add broccolini and wine. Turn up heat and continue cooking and
stirring until broccolini is tender-crisp and most of the wine has
evaporated.

Season with salt and pepper to taste.

Prep = 5 minutes   **Cook** = 8 to 10 minutes   **Yield** = 4 to 6 servings

Diane's Poached Figs Pinot Noir

Diane Jacobsen, a Connecticut local, is a big fan
of poached figs. Her recipe makes an excellent side dish
to pork, duck, and poultry. Whatever variety of figs are
bought must be ripe, but not so ripe
that the skins are splitting.

1 bottle (750 m) Pinot Noir
1 cup (340 g) honey
½ cup (120 ml) red wine vinegar
1 teaspoon whole peppercorns
1 cinnamon stick
2 teaspoons whole cloves, tied in a cheesecloth bag
2 pounds (905 g) fresh figs, halved
½ teaspoon salt

In a nonreactive saucepan, bring the wine, honey, vinegar, peppercorns, cinnamon stick, and bag of cloves to a simmer. Continue
cooking at a low simmer until the mixture is reduced to light
syrup, 30 to 40 minutes. Remove from heat. Strain the mixture
and return it to the saucepan. Add the halved figs and salt; stir
gently. Cook over low heat until the figs are just tender, 5 to 10
minutes. Remove from heat. Using a slotted spoon, transfer the
figs to a bowl. There should be about 1 cup (240 ml) Pinot Noir
syrup in the saucepan; if there is more, boil it down to reduce to 1
cup (240 ml). Remove syrup from the heat and let cool. When
cool, add the figs back to the syrup and refrigerate.

Serve the figs cold, with the syrup spooned over them.

Prep = 10 minutes   **Cook** = 35 to 55 minutes   **Yield** = 6 servings

New Potatoes
with White Zinfandel

Alchemy happens to potatoes when they are simmered in wine. These new potatoes are first cooked in White Zinfandel before sautéing in butter and herbs. They make the perfect accompaniment for any seafood dish.

12 small scrubbed new potatoes
 2 cups (475 ml) White Zinfandel
 3 tablespoons 42 g) butter
 1 clove garlic, crushed
 1 shallot, minced
 1 tablespoon (4 g) minced fresh dill
 1 tablespoon (4 g) minced fresh parsley
    Salt and pepper

Use a vegetable peeler to peel a strip of skin off around the sides of each potato. Put potatoes and wine in a medium saucepan and bring to a boil. Reduce heat to medium, cover, and cook until potatoes are tender (about 30 minutes). Drain off the liquid from potatoes in a colander. In a medium skillet over medium heat, melt butter and sauté garlic and shallot until tender (about 4 minutes). Turn down heat; add potatoes, dill, and parsley, then gently shake around in pan to coat with butter. Season to taste with salt and pepper.

Prep = 15 minutes   **Cook** = 40 to 45 minutes   **Yield** = 4 servings

Garlic and Wine Mashed Potatoes

The magic of these mashed potatoes is in cooking the potatoes in wine instead of water. This notable technique of flavoring the cooking water creates a truly transcendent mashed potato experience.

- 2 pounds (905 g) Idaho potatoes, peeled and cubed
- 2 cups (475 ml) dry white wine
- 2 cloves garlic, peeled and sliced in half
- 4 tablespoons (55 g) butter
- ¼ cup (58 g) sour cream
- ½ cup (120 ml) milk, heated
- 1 tablespoon (4 g) minced fresh chives (optional)
  Salt and pepper

Place potatoes in a large saucepan and add wine and garlic. Add enough water to the pan to cover potatoes. Bring to a boil, then reduce heat slightly and cook for 20 to 30 minutes, or until tender. Drain potatoes well in a colander. Remove garlic cloves. Be sure saucepan is completely dry and melt butter in it over low heat. Remove from heat and return warm potatoes to the saucepan. Begin mashing with a handheld potato masher. Add sour cream, hot milk, and chives. Season to taste with salt and pepper. Continue mashing until no longer lumpy.

Prep = 15 minutes   **Cook** = 40 to 50 minutes   **Yield** = 4 servings

Madeira-Glazed Carrots

Eating this dish is like eating sweet little orange coins of carrot "candy." Madeira creates a grown-up version of this treat. This is a great side dish for seasonal meals featuring just about any type of roast.

1 dozen medium-size carrots, peeled and cut into 1-inch (2.5-cm) lengths
4 tablespoons (55 g) butter
⅓ cup (75 g) firmly packed brown sugar
1 teaspoon ginger
3 tablespoons (45 ml) Madeira wine

Place carrots in a large saucepan and cover with water. Bring to a boil. Reduce heat and simmer for 20 to 30 minutes, or until tender. Drain well. Melt butter in a large saucepan over medium heat. Blend in brown sugar, ginger, and Madeira. Bring to boil and cook for 1 minute, until bubbling. Toss carrots in glaze.

Prep = 10 minutes   **Cook** = 30 to 40 minutes   **Yield** = 6 servings

Madeira-Maple Baked Acorn Squash

Of all winter squashes, acorn squash has the richest, most buttery taste. The bowl-shaped squash halves are perfect vessels for melted butter and brown sugar or any other sweet toppings.

- 2 medium-size acorn squash, split in half and seeds and fiber removed
- 3 tablespoons (42 g) butter
- 3 tablespoons (45 ml) Madeira wine
- ¼ cup (60 ml) maple syrup
- ¼ cup (60 ml) heavy cream

Preheat oven to 350°F (180°C, or gas mark 4). Place squash in an ungreased 9 × 13-inch (22.5 × 32.5-inch) baking pan, cut side up. In a small saucepan, over medium heat, bring butter, Madeira, maple syrup, and cream to a boil. Boil for 1 minute and remove from heat. Pour one-fourth of mixture into the cavity of each acorn squash. Bake, uncovered, for 1 hour, basting the cut edges of the squash with the glaze from the center every 15 minutes. Squash halves may be sliced in half again for smaller portions.

Prep = 10 minutes   **Cook** = 1 hour, 5 minutes
Yield = 4 to 8 servings

Risotto
Pinot Grigio

The process of cooking risotto is different
from that of other rice dishes. It requires continuous
stirring as part of the "nurturing" process. The effort
is well worth the end result.

1 tablespoon (14 g) butter
2 tablespoons (30 ml) olive oil
2 shallots, minced
1 tablespoon (4 g) fresh minced parsley
1 cup (195 g) uncooked Arborio rice
2 ½ cups (570 ml) warmed chicken broth
   Pinch of saffron (optional)
1 cup (240 ml) Pinot Grigio or other white wine
½ cup (50 g) freshly grated Parmesan cheese
¼ teaspoon coarsely ground black pepper
   Salt

In a medium nonstick skillet, melt butter and olive oil. Sauté shallots and parsley in the pan until tender (about 5 minutes). Stir in
rice and sauté until edges are translucent. Add ½ cup (120 ml)
chicken broth and saffron, stirring constantly until liquid is
absorbed. Reduce heat to medium and add wine. Cook, uncovered,
for 5 minutes, stirring frequently, until wine is absorbed. Repeat
process with 1 cup (240 ml) chicken broth until it's absorbed, then
add remaining cup of chicken broth until that is absorbed. Stir in
cheese and pepper. If desired, add additional salt to taste.

Prep = 10 minutes   **Cook** = 35 to 40 minutes
Yield = 4 servings

Sautéed Polenta

Polenta can be served straight from the saucepan,
or it can be chilled until it's set, then sliced and sautéed.
The first is more like grits, and the second is
molded and sliced into squares or triangles
before being sautéed or grilled.

1	cup (140 g) yellow cornmeal
¾	cup (175 ml) dry white wine
3 ¼	cups (770 ml) boiling water
½	teaspoon salt
	All-purpose flour, for dredging
2	tablespoons (28 g) butter

In a 2-quart (1.9-L) saucepan, mix cornmeal and wine. Blend in boiling water and salt. Cook over medium heat, stirring constantly, until mixture thickens and boils 8 to 10 minutes). Reduce heat to low, cover and simmer for 10 minutes, stirring occasionally, until very thick. Remove from heat and stir until smooth. (At this point, polenta may be served directly on the plate as a side dish.)

Spray a 9 × 5-inch (22.5 × 13-cm) loaf pan with nonstick cooking spray. Pour polenta into pan; cover with plastic wrap and chill for 12 hours or until firm. Unmold and cut into ½-inch (1.3-cm) slices. Lightly coat slices with flour. Melt butter in a medium nonstick skillet over low heat and sauté slices for 5 minutes on each side until browned.

Serve warm as a side dish in place of pasta, rice, or potatoes.

Prep = 5 minutes **Cook** = 30 minutes **Chill** = 12 hours
Yield = 6 servings

Sherry Glazed Sweet Potatoes with Pecans

This side dish is likely to become
more popular than dessert whenever it appears
on the menu. Some might marvel at why it can't be
(or just hasn't yet been) served à la mode!

2 pounds (905 g) sweet potatoes
3 tablespoons (42 g) butter
⅓ cup (75 g) brown sugar
3 tablespoons (45 ml) sherry
1 teaspoon grated orange peel
¼ teaspoon salt
⅔ cup (65 g) toasted pecans, coarsely chopped*

Place sweet potatoes in a large saucepan and bring to a boil.
Cover and simmer for 20 to 25 minutes, or until tender when
pierced with a fork. Cool potatoes and slip out of skins. Cut into
½-inch (1.3 cm) slices. In a medium skillet, over medium heat, melt
butter and add sugar, sherry, orange peel, and salt. Stir until
smooth and bubbling. Gently stir in pecans and sweet potatoes,
taking care not to break them up.

*To toast pecans: Preheat oven to 350°F (180°C, or gas mark 4)
and spread pecans on a baking sheet. Bake for 6 to 8 minutes,
stirring once or twice, until evenly golden brown. Watch carefully
to avoid burning.

Variation: Mashed sweet potatoes: Reduce brown sugar to ¼ cup
(60 g) and omit pecans. After adding sweet potato slices to the
skillet, mash with a potato masher.

Prep = 15 minutes   **Cook** = 35 to 40 minutes
Yield = 6 servings

Summer Squash Sauté

Yellow squash is a perennial bumper crop in
most gardens. Somehow, it seems to be the only
vegetable in the garden that squirrels won't eat. This
simple preparation assures this recipe
will become a summer standby.

1 tablespoon (14 g) butter
1 tablespoon (15 ml) olive oil
1 clove garlic, crushed
4 yellow squash (about 2 pounds, or 905 g, total)
⅓ cup (80 ml) dry white wine
2 tablespoons (22 g) chopped pimiento
¼ cup (25 g) grated Parmesan cheese
   Salt and pepper

In a medium nonstick skillet over medium heat, melt butter and
oil with garlic. Add squash and wine. Cook, stirring frequently, until
most of the wine has evaporated and squash is still tender-crisp.
Toss with pimiento and cheese. Season with salt and pepper
to taste.

Prep = 10 minutes **Cook** = 10 minutes **Yield** = 4 servings

Brunch Dishes

Eggs Sardou
Chablis

This rich, indulgent dish was originally served
at Antoine's in New Orleans. Many versions of eggs
Sardou feature creamed spinach but sautéing
the spinach with bits of ham and white wine
creates an equally refined result.

2 tablespoons (28 g) butter
1 clove garlic
1 shallot, minced
½ cup (75 g) chopped baked ham
¼ cup (60 ml) Chablis
1 pound (455 g) baby spinach
4 whole artichoke bottoms, leaves trimmed and boiled
4 poached eggs

HOLLANDAISE:
1 tablespoon (15 ml) lemon juice
1 tablespoon (15 ml) Chablis
3 egg yolks
1 stick (¼ pound, or 112 g) butter, cut into tablespoons

Melt butter in a nonstick skillet with garlic, shallot, and chopped
ham and sauté until ham is lightly browned. Add wine and reduce
liquid to about half. Add spinach and continue cooking and stirring
until spinach is limp. Fill artichoke bottoms with spinach mixture.
Top with poached eggs and hollandaise.

For Hollandaise: Put lemon juice and wine in a mixing bowl that
fits over a saucepan of simmering water (water should not boil or
touch the bottom). Add egg yolks and beat with a wire whisk until
thick and lemon colored. Add half of butter and keep whisking
until butter is melted. Add remaining butter and continue stirring
vigorously until butter is melted and sauce has thickened. (If
sauce begins to curdle, it can be resurrected by vigorously beating
in a tablespoon of lemon juice or putting curdled sauce in the
blender). Remove bowl from water and set to the side of the stove
so as not to continue cooking or get too cold.

Prep = 20 minutes   **Cook** = 30 to 35 minutes
Yield = 2 to 4 servings

Ham and Cheddar Brunch Casserole

This brunch casserole has many familiar variations but the essential concept is a breakfast-style bread-and-cheese pudding. It's prepared a day ahead, eliminating any last-minute fuss. Sherry and grape tomatoes grace this version.

- 6 large eggs
- 1 cup (240 ml) milk
- ½ cup (120 ml) sherry
- ½ cup (120 ml) half-and-half
- ½ teaspoon dry mustard
- 1 teaspoon Worcestershire sauce
  Dash of red pepper sauce (optional)
- 2 cups (300 g) chopped baked ham
- 2 cups (225 g) grated Cheddar cheese
- ½ cup (50 g) sliced scallions
- 2 cups (70 g) bread cubes
- 12 grape tomatoes, sliced into 4 thin slices each
- ¼ cup (25 g) grated Parmesan cheese
  Paprika

Preheat oven to 300°F (150°C, or gas mark 2) and spray a 9 × 13-inch (22.5 × 32.5-cm) glass baking dish with cooking spray. In a large mixing bowl, beat eggs, milk, sherry, half-and-half, Worcestershire sauce, and red pepper sauce with a wire whisk until blended. Stir in ham, Cheddar cheese, scallions, and bread cubes. Spread into baking dish and arrange tomatoes over the top. Sprinkle with Parmesan cheese and paprika. Cover and refrigerate for 24 hours. Bake for 1 hour and 10 minutes, until puffy and golden brown. Let stand for 10 minutes before slicing.

Prep = 20 minutes   **Chill** = 24 hours   **Cook** = 1 hour, 20 minutes
Yield = 8 servings

Ham and Vermouth Vegetable Frittata

A frittata is a wonderful cross between an
omelet and a quiche. There is little need for advanced
preparation, and the touch of vermouth sets the
morning off to a refined start.

4 eggs
3 tablespoons (45 ml) vermouth
2 tablespoons (30 ml) heavy cream
2 tablespoons (12 g) grated Parmesan cheese
¼ teaspoon salt
  Pinch of cracked pepper
2 tablespoons (8 g) minced fresh chives
1 tablespoon (14 g) butter
1 tablespoon (15 ml) olive oil
½ cup (75 g) thinly sliced and seeded red bell pepper
½ cup (80 g) thinly sliced onion
1 cup (70 g) sliced mushrooms
½ cup (60 g) chopped zucchini
1 cup (150 g) chopped ham
2 plum tomatoes, sliced
½ cup (60 g) shredded Asiago or Monterrey Jack cheese

In a mixing bowl, beat eggs, vermouth, heavy cream, Parmesan
cheese, salt, pepper, and 1 tablespoon chives with a wire whisk
until well blended.

In a nonstick 10-inch (25-cm) skillet, melt butter and olive oil
over medium heat. Sauté bell pepper, onion, mushrooms, zucchini,
and ham until vegetables are tender-crisp (3 to 5 minutes). Pour
egg mixture over the ham mixture in the skillet. Cook over medium heat, stirring gently until eggs are almost set (6 to 8 minutes).
Reduce heat to low and top with tomato slices, cheese, and
remaining chives. Cover and cook for 2 to 3 minutes longer, or
until eggs are completely set. Cut into wedges and serve.

Prep = 20 minutes **Cook** = 18 to 20 minutes
Yield = 4 servings

Artichoke and Portobello Mushroom Quiche

This is not your ordinary quiche recipe.
Typically, the mixture of cream, eggs, and cheese
is simply poured into an unbaked pie shell. I find that
process always produces heavy custard and a doughy crust.
In my version, I make a cheese sauce and chill the filling
first. When the liquid has been bound into a sauce,
the end result is a flakier crust.

6 tablespoons (84 g) butter

2 portobello mushroom caps, chopped coarsely

⅓ cup (53 g) minced onion

⅓ cup (80 ml) sherry

1 package (10 ounces, 280 g) frozen artichoke hearts,
cooked according to package directions

¼ cup (31 g) all-purpose flour

1 cup (240 ml) milk

1 cup (240 ml) half-and-half

2 cups (200 g) grated Asiago cheese

¼ cup (25 g) grated Parmesan cheese

Salt and pepper

4 eggs, beaten

1 roll of refrigerated piecrust (do not use a frozen pie shell)

Prep = 35 minutes   **Cook** = 40 to 50 minutes
Yield = 6 to 8 servings

Melt 2 tablespoons (28 g) butter in a small nonstick skillet over medium-high heat. Sauté mushrooms and onion until tender (about 5 minutes). Add sherry and reduce until most of the liquid has evaporated. Toss gently with artichokes, transfer to a bowl. Cover and chill in refrigerator.

Meanwhile, melt remaining 4 tablespoons (55 g) butter in a medium saucepan over medium heat and blend in flour until smooth and bubbling. Blend in milk and half-and-half with a wire whisk and cook, stirring constantly, until thickened and boiling. Blend in Asiago cheese and Parmesan cheese until melted. Season with salt and pepper to taste. Beat in eggs. Pour into a bowl, cover, and chill. Unroll pastry crust and fit into a 10-inch (25-cm) quiche pan, springform pan, or deep-dish pie plate. Chill in refrigerator.

Preheat oven to 400°F (200°C, or gas mark 6). Place pan on a baking sheet. Fill with mushroom mixture. Spread cheese sauce over that and bake for 40 to 50 minutes, or until golden brown and puffy on top and filling is set. Cool for 20 minutes before slicing.

Brunch Scramble Benedict

This dish is missing the poached eggs and hollandaise sauce, but it's a no-fuss way to create the Benedict effect. The asparagus and cheese sauce can be prepared the night before and reheated before serving.

4   English muffins, split in half, toasted, and lightly buttered
8   slices grilled Canadian bacon
24 asparagus spears, cooked until tender
2   tablespoons (28 g) butter
12 eggs, beaten
    Paprika

CHEDDAR CHIVE SAUCE:
4   tablespoons (55 g) butter
¼   cup (31 g) all-purpose flour
1   cup (240 ml) milk
⅔   cup (160 ml) half-and-half
½   cup (120 ml) dry white wine
1   tablespoon (4 g) minced chives
½   cup (60 g) grated Cheddar cheese
2   tablespoons (10 g) grated Parmesan cheese
    Salt and pepper

Prep = 20 minutes   **Cook** = 20 minutes   **Yield** = 4 servings

Arrange 2 English muffin halves on each serving plate, top each with a slice of Canadian bacon and 3 asparagus spears. Melt butter in a large nonstick skillet over medium heat. Pour eggs into skillet. As mixture begins to set at bottom and side, gently lift cooked portions from the bottom so that thin, uncooked portion can flow to the bottom. (When scrambling eggs, avoid constant stirring.) Cook for 3 to 4 minutes, or until eggs are thickened throughout and still moist. Spoon scrambled eggs over asparagus, evenly distributed, and top with sauce and dust with paprika.

For Cheddar Chive Sauce: In a medium saucepan over medium heat, melt butter and blend in flour, stirring with a wire whisk until bubbling. Gradually blend in milk, half-and-half, wine, and chives. Heat to boiling while stirring constantly with a wire whisk until thickened. Boil for 1 minute, remove from heat, and stir in cheeses. Stir until cheese melts and season with salt and pepper to taste.

Ham and Asparagus Rolls Mornay

Mornay sauce takes on many different nuances depending on the cheese and formula used. A touch of sherry and egg yolks achieves a golden glaze for any gratin dish.

4	dozen asparagus spears, cooked tender-crisp
8	large slices baked ham, about ⅛-inch (3-mm) thick (a deli can do this for you)
⅓	cup (80 ml) sherry
⅓	cup (80 ml) heavy cream
2	egg yolks
1	onion, cut in half
1	cup (240 ml) chicken stock
1	cup (240 ml) half-and-half
4	tablespoons (55 g) butter
¼	cup (31 g) all-purpose flour
¼	teaspoon salt
	Pinch grated nutmeg
¾	cup (90 g) shredded Swiss or Asiago cheese
¾	cup (75 g) grated Parmesan cheese

Divide asparagus spears evenly among ham slices (about 6 spears per slice) and roll up ham. Arrange rolls in a 9 × 13-inch (22.5 × 32.5-cm) casserole dish or put two rolls, side by side, in individual casserole dishes. Beat sherry, heavy cream, and egg yolks together in a small bowl and set aside. Put onion in a large saucepan and pour chicken stock and half-and-half over the top. Bring to a simmer and remove from heat (this draws out the onion juice). Remove onion.

In another large saucepan, melt butter and blend in flour, salt, and nutmeg over medium heat. Cook, stirring constantly, with a wire whisk to make a smooth, bubbling roux. Blend in chicken stock mixture and cream mixture. Continue cooking and stirring until mixture is thickened and bubbling. Blend in ½ cup (60 g) Swiss cheese and ½ cup (50 g) Parmesan cheese until smooth and melted. Pour over ham rolls and top with remaining cheese. Preheat oven to 450°F (230°C, or gas mark 8) and bake for 8 to 12 minutes, or until cheese is golden brown and puffy.

Prep = 20 minutes   **Cook** = 30 to 35 minutes   **Yield** = 4 Servings

The Gourmet's Guide to Cooking with Wine

Scotch Eggs with Dilly Cream Sauce

Like many British breakfast dishes, this is a rich way to start off the morning.

1   pound (455 g) herb-seasoned breakfast sausage
6   hard-cooked eggs, chilled and peeled
½   cup (63 g) all-purpose flour
2   eggs, beaten
1   cup (115 g) fine dry bread crumbs
    Vegetable oil, for frying

DILLY CREAM SAUCE:
4   tablespoons (55 g) butter
1   shallot, minced
¼   cup (31 g) all-purpose flour
1   cup (240 ml) milk
½   cup (120 ml) half-and-half
½   cup (120 ml) white wine
1   tablespoon (4 g) minced fresh dill

Divide sausage into 6 portions. Roll each egg in flour and mold a portion of sausage around each egg. Dip sausage-wrapped eggs into beaten egg and roll in bread crumbs. Heat vegetable oil to 350°F (180°C, or gas mark 4). Fry each egg in oil for 4 to 5 minutes, or until sausage is cooked and crust is golden brown. Drain well and serve with Dilly Cream Sauce.

For Dilly Cream Sauce: Melt butter in a nonstick medium saucepan over medium-high heat. Sauté shallot in butter until soft (about 3 minutes). Blend in flour and stir with a wire whisk until smooth and bubbling. Blend in milk, half-and-half, wine, and fresh dill. Cook, stirring constantly, until thickened and smooth.

Prep = 30 minutes   **Cook** = 25 to 30 minutes   **Yield** = 6 servings

Filet Mignon Benedict with Cabernet Béarnaise

The Cabernet Béarnaise sauce makes this
Filet Mignon Benedict unique and converts any
weekend morning into a major holiday. That said, why
serve this just for brunch? It makes a great
supper dish as well.

½	cup (120 ml) Cabernet Sauvignon or other red wine
1	tablespoon (15 ml) tarragon vinegar
4	large egg yolks
10	tablespoons (140 g) butter, cut into cubes
1	tablespoon (4 g) fresh minced chives
4	large portobello mushroom caps
2	tablespoons (30 ml) garlic-flavored oil
	Salt
2	tablespoons (28 g) butter
2	tablespoons (30 ml) dry vermouth
4	small filets mignons (about 4 ounces, 115 g, each)
2	English muffins, split in half, toasted, and buttered
4	poached eggs

Prep = 20 minutes   **Cook** = 40 minutes   **Yield** = 4 servings

In a small saucepan, bring wine and vinegar to a boil and reduce to about 3 tablespoons (45 ml) liquid. Transfer to a mixing bowl that fits over a saucepan of simmering water (water should not boil or touch the bottom). Beat egg yolks into wine mixture with a wire whisk. Add 5 tablespoons (70 g) butter and keep whisking until butter is melted. Add 5 tablespoons (70 g) more butter and continue stirring vigorously until butter is melted and sauce has thickened. Blend in chives. If sauce begins to curdle, it can be res-urrected by vigorously beating in a tablespoon of boiling water. Remove bowl from water and set to the side of the stove so as not to continue cooking or get too cold.

Brush portobello mushroom caps and filets with garlic-flavored olive oil. Lightly season with salt. In a large, nonstick skillet, melt 1 tablespoon (14 g) butter and sauté mushroom caps on both sides until tender (about 8 minutes). Deglaze pan with vermouth until evaporated and set aside. In another nonstick skillet, heat remain-ing butter until melted and sauté filets (about 3 minutes on both sides) until medium rare.

Assemble on plates by topping each English muffin half with a portobello mushroom cap topped with a filet mignon. Spoon sauce over top.

Sherry Pain Perdu

Pain perdu, or "lost bread," is a breakfast and brunch favorite in New Orleans. The idea is that restaurants could revive stale French bread from the previous night. For pralines, I use the candied pecans available in green foil bags.

3 large eggs
½ cup (120 ml) half-and-half
¼ cup (60 ml) sherry
1 tablespoon (13 g) sugar
½ teaspoon vanilla extract
¼ teaspoon salt
8 slices French bread (cut 1 inch, or 2.5 cm, thick)
1 to 2 tablespoons (14 to 28 g) butter
Confectioners' sugar
Candied pecans
Maple syrup

ORANGE BUTTER:
1 stick (¼ pound, or 112 g) butter, softened
1 teaspoon grated orange peel

Beat eggs in a large mixing bowl with half-and-half, sherry, sugar, vanilla, and salt. Dip bread slices in egg batter. Melt 1 tablespoon (14 g) butter in a nonstick skillet or griddle and sauté bread on each side until golden (about 4 minutes on each side). Use additional butter if needed. Dust with confectioners' sugar and sprinkle with candied pecans. Serve with warm maple syrup and scoops of Orange Butter.

To make Orange Butter: Beat softened butter with grated orange peel.

Prep = 20 minutes   **Cook** = 15 minutes   **Yield** = 4 servings

Desserts

Apple Crisp with Sherry Cream Sauce

This apple crisp recipe lends itself well to multiplying for serving dozens of people. Cutting firm butter into flour and brown sugar can be exhausting. Stirring in melted butter makes this a breeze. Apple crisp can always be served with ice cream, but the sherry cream sauce adds a delightful Old English touch.

- 1 cup (200 g) sugar
- ½ teaspoon ground cinnamon
- ⅓ cup (42 g) all-purpose flour
- 6 Cortland apples, peeled, cored, and sliced
- 2 tablespoons (28 g) butter, melted

CRUMB TOPPING:
- 1 cup (125 g) all-purpose flour
- 1 cup (225 g) firmly packed brown sugar
- ½ cup (40 g) rolled oats
- ¾ cup (85 g) toasted, chopped pecans*
- 1 stick (¼ pound, or 112 g) butter, melted

SHERRY CREAM SAUCE:
- ⅓ cup (80 ml) sherry
- 1 large egg
- 1 teaspoon vanilla extract
- 1 cup (200 g) sugar
- ½ cup (112 g) butter, melted and cooled slightly
- 1 cup (240 ml) heavy cream, whipped

Preheat oven to 375°F (190°C, or gas mark 5). Combine sugar, flour, and cinnamon in a large mixing bowl. Add apples and stir until coated with sugar mixture. Use melted butter to grease a 3-quart (2.8-L) baking dish or casserole. Spoon apples into dish and cover with Crumb Topping. Bake for 35 to 45 minutes, or until apples are bubbling and the topping is golden brown.

For Crumb Topping: Combine flour, brown sugar, rolled oats, and pecans in a medium mixing bowl. Stir melted butter into dry mixture.

For Sherry Cream Sauce: Beat sherry, egg, and vanilla together in a small saucepan. Blend in sugar and butter. Bring to a boil over medium heat, stirring constantly with a wire whisk until smooth and slightly thickened. Pour into a bowl and cover with plastic wrap. Chill for at least 4 hours. Fold into whipped cream. Note: This sauce freezes well for future use. It makes an excellent topping for fresh fruit.

*To toast pecans: Preheat oven to 350°F (180°C, or gas mark 4) and spread pecans on a baking sheet. Bake for 6 to 8 minutes, stirring once or twice until evenly golden brown. Watch carefully to avoid burning.

Prep = 25 minutes   **Cook** = 1 hour, 10 minutes
Chill = 4 hours   **Yield** = 8 servings

Almond Sherry Bars

These make a wonderful addition to any
tea-party tray as well as an excellent holiday bar for a
cookie exchange. These are similar to lemon squares,
without the lemon juice or peel. The tops can be
garnished with slivers of candied cherries.

- 1 cup (125 g) all-purpose flour
- 1 stick (¼ pound, or 112 g) butter, softened
- ¼ cup (30 g) powdered sugar
- 1 teaspoon almond extract
- 2 large eggs
- 1 cup (200 g) granulated sugar
- 2 tablespoons (30 ml) sherry
- ½ teaspoon baking powder
- ¼ teaspoon salt
- ⅔ cup (73 g) toasted slivered almonds*
  Additional powdered sugar

Preheat oven to 350°F (180°C, or gas mark 4). In a medium bowl, mix flour, butter, confectioners' sugar, and almond extract until blended. Press into an 8- or 9-inch (20- or 22.5-cm) square pan, building up ½ inch (1.3 cm) on the edges. Bake for 20 minutes and remove crust from oven.

In a medium mixing bowl, beat eggs, sugar, sherry, baking powder, and salt on high speed for 3 minutes, until light and fluffy. Stir in almonds. Pour over crust and bake for 25 to 30 minutes until no indentation remains when touched lightly in the center. Cool completely on a wire rack for 1 hour. Dust with additional confectioners' sugar and cut bars into 5 rows of 5.

*To toast almonds: Preheat oven to 350°F (180°C, or gas mark 4) and spread almonds on a baking sheet. Toast for 6 to 8 minutes, turning once or twice until evenly golden brown. Watch carefully to avoid burning.

Prep = 15 minutes **Cook** = 50 to 56 minutes **Yield** = 25 bars

Cherry Wine Dumplings Amandine

This dessert can almost substitute as a breakfast/brunch dish if served with a little whipped honey butter instead of ice cream. The secret to making dumplings is not to peek at them until they are ready. Resist the temptation to lift the lid and watch them take shape.

- 2 bags (16 ounces, 455 g, each) frozen dark sweet cherries
- ⅓ cup (67 g) sugar
- ⅓ cup (80 ml) black cherry wine
- ¼ teaspoon almond extract

DUMPLING BATTER:
- 1 cup (125 g) all-purpose flour
- 2 teaspoons baking powder
- ¼ teaspoon salt
- ¾ cup (175 ml) whole milk
- ¼ teaspoon almond extract
- ¼ teaspoon ground cinnamon mixed with 1 tablespoon (13 g) sugar
  Vanilla ice cream
- ½ cup (60 g) toasted chopped almonds*

Prep = 15 minutes   **Cook** = 20 to 25 minutes   **Yield** = 6 servings

Combine cherries, sugar, cherry wine, and almond in a large skillet. Bring to a boil over high heat and reduce until syrupy (10 to 12 minutes). Reduce heat to medium low. Spoon dumpling batter in about 18 tablespoonfuls over simmering cherries and sprinkle with cinnamon mixture.

Cover skillet and simmer gently until dumplings are set and dry to touch (10 to 12 minutes). Serve warm, with ice cream sprinkled with toasted almonds.

To make Dumpling Batter: In small bowl, stir together flour, baking powder, and salt with a fork. Combine milk with almond extract and gradually stir into flour mixture, just until a wet dough forms (don't overmix).

*To toast almonds: Preheat oven to 350°F (180°C, or gas mark 4) and spread almonds on a baking sheet. Toast for 6 to 8 minutes, turning once or twice until evenly golden brown. Watch carefully to avoid burning.

Classic Tiramisu

In Italian, *tiramisu* literally means "pick me up."
The classic version is laced with Marsala, although
there are many variations.

6	large egg yolks
¾	cup (150 g) sugar
⅔	cup (160 ml) milk
1	pound (455 g) mascarpone cheese
½	teaspoon vanilla extract
⅓	cup (80 ml) espresso or very strong coffee, cooled
1	tablespoon (15 g) firmly packed brown sugar
¼	cup (60 ml) Marsala wine
2	packages (3 ounces, or 85 g, each) ladyfingers
1¼	cups (150 g) whipping cream, whipped to stiff peaks
	Cocoa

In a medium saucepan, beat egg yolks and sugar with a wire whisk, then blend in milk. Heat to boiling over medium heat, stirring constantly; reduce heat to low. Boil, stirring, for 1 minute, then remove from heat. Pour into medium bowl and place plastic wrap directly on surface of the custard mixture. Refrigerate for at least 2 hours, until chilled.

Blend mascarpone cheese and vanilla into custard with an electric mixer. In a separate bowl, combine espresso, brown sugar, and Marsala. Separate ladyfingers and brush cut side with espresso mixture. Arrange half of ladyfingers (cut side up) in an 7 × 11-inch (17.5 × 27.5-cm) glass baking dish. Spread half of cheese mixture over ladyfingers, followed by half of whipped cream. Repeat layers with remaining ladyfingers, cheese mixture, and whipped cream. Sprinkle with cocoa. Refrigerate for at least 4 hours before serving, but not longer than 24 hours.

Prep = 30 minutes   **Cook** = 10 minutes
Chill = 2 hours plus 4 to 6 hours   **Yield** = 8 servings

Devonshire Cream Strawberry Trifle

Devonshire cream is rich and slightly tangy, almost like cream fraîche. Similar results can be achieved by adding a touch of sour cream when whipping heavy cream.

½ cup (160 g) strawberry jam
2 quarts (1.1 L) fresh strawberries, hulled and cut in half
1 pint (2 cups, or 475 ml) whipping cream
¼ cup (80 g) sour cream
⅓ cup (40 g) confectioners' sugar
1 teaspoon vanilla extract
1 pound cake (10 or 12 ounces, or 280 or 340 g)

SHERRY SYRUP:
¼ cup (60 ml) water
½ cup (100 g) granulated sugar
⅓ cup (80 ml) sherry

PASTRY CREAM:
2 packages (3 ounces, or 85 g, each) vanilla pudding mix (regular, not instant)
4 cups (945 ml) half-and-half
6 tablespoons (84 g) butter
1 tablespoon (15 ml) vanilla extract

⅓ cup (30 g) toasted sliced almonds*

Prep = 35 minutes   **Cook** = 20 minutes   **Chill** = 4 hours
Yield = 6 to 8 servings

Stir strawberry jam with a fork to loosen it up and then add strawberries. Gently toss berries until they are coated with jam. Combine whipping cream, sour cream, confectioners' sugar, and vanilla extract in a large mixing bowl and beat until peaks that are stiff but not dry form.

Slice pound cake into 12 slices and then cut each slice into 6 cubes. Arrange one-third of pound cake in the bottom of a trifle bowl or large soufflé dish. Using a pastry brush, brush cubes with sherry syrup. Top with one-third of strawberries followed by one-third of pastry cream and one-third of whipping cream. Repeat layering, ending with whipping cream, and sprinkle with toasted almonds. Cover with plastic wrap and refrigerate for 3 hours before serving but not longer than 24 hours.

For Sherry Syrup: Bring water, granulated sugar, and sherry to a boil. Cool to room temperature.

For Pastry Cream: Prepare pudding mix according to package directions, substituting half-and-half for milk. Once thickened, remove from heat and whisk in butter until melted and smooth. Transfer to a bowl and press plastic wrap over the surface of cream. Chill for at least 4 hours.

*To toast almonds: Preheat oven to 350°F (180°C, or gas mark 4) and spread almonds on a baking sheet. Bake for 6 to 8 minutes, stirring once or twice, until evenly golden brown. Watch carefully to avoid burning.

Nutcracker Sherry Cake

Unlike the much maligned (and often unfairly so)
fruitcake that lingers for years in the same can, this holiday
gift doesn't last long at all … because it is quickly eaten.

2 cups (250 g) all-purpose flour
1 cup (120 g) crushed graham cracker crumbs
1 cup (225 g) firmly packed brown sugar
1 teaspoon baking powder
1 teaspoon baking soda
½ teaspoon ground cinnamon
2 sticks (½ pound, or 225 g) butter, softened
½ cup (120 ml) orange juice
½ cup (120 ml) sherry
1 tablespoon (6 g) grated orange peel
3 eggs
1¼ cups (138 g) toasted chopped pecans*

GLAZE:
2 tablespoons (30 g) brown sugar
1 tablespoon (15 ml) half-and-half
1 tablespoon (15 ml) sherry
1 tablespoon (14 g) butter
¾ cup (94 g) confectioners' sugar

Preheat oven to 350°F (180°C, or gas mark 4). Grease and flour a 12-cup (2.8-L) Bundt cake or 10-inch (25-cm) tube pan. In a large mixing bowl combine flour, graham cracker crumbs, sugar, baking powder, baking soda, cinnamon, butter, orange juice, sherry, orange peel, and eggs. Beat for 3 minutes at medium speed. Stir in 1 cup (125 g) pecans by hand. Bake for 40 to 50 minutes, or until a toothpick inserted in the center comes out clean. Cool upright for 15 minutes, then invert onto serving plate. Cool for at least another hour before glazing. Drizzle Glaze over the top and sides of cake. Sprinkle with remaining pecans.

For Glaze: In a small saucepan, combine brown sugar, half-and-half, and sherry. Cook over low heat just until sugar is dissolved and blend in confectioners' sugar.

*To toast pecans: Preheat oven to 350°F (180°C, or gas mark 4) and spread pecans on a baking sheet. Bake for 6 to 8 minutes, stirring once or twice, until evenly golden brown. Watch carefully to avoid burning.

Prep = 35 minutes   **Cook** = 40 to 50 minutes
Yield = 12 to 16 servings

Peach Melba
Pinot Noir

In 1892, Auguste Escoffier invented peach
Melba at the Savoy Hotel in London. Legend
has it that it was to honor Australian opera soprano,
Dame Nellie Melba. Pinot Noir wine adds an
interesting dimension to this classic dessert.

- 1 cup (240 ml) Pinot Noir
- 1 cup (320 g) seedless black raspberry preserves
- 6 ripe freestone peaches
- 1 quart (945 ml) peach or vanilla ice cream

Combine Pinot Noir and raspberry preserves in a small saucepan.
Bring to a boil over high heat, reduce heat to low, and simmer for
about 5 minutes. Remove from heat and chill for at least 3 hours.

Peel and pit peaches, split in half, and arrange 2 halves in each
of 6 dessert bowls. Top with a scoop of ice cream in each. Spoon
sauce over ice cream and serve immediately.

Prep = 15 minutes   **Cook** = 5 minutes   **Yield** = 6 servings

Mixed Berries Merlot

A mixture of berries is an ideal summer dessert.
This syrup can be made ahead of time and kept in the
refrigerator. For a quick and easy dessert, buy berries from
the grocery store with the rest of dinner's ingredients.

- 3 ½ cups (830 ml) Merlot
- ⅔ cup (134 g) sugar
- 1 thick orange slice
- 1 thin lemon slice
- ½ vanilla bean, split in half lengthwise
- 2 cups (250 g) fresh raspberries
- 1 cup (145 g) fresh blueberries
- 1 cup (145 g) fresh blackberries
- 1 quart (945 ml) vanilla ice cream

Combine Merlot, sugar, orange slice, lemon slice, and vanilla bean in a large saucepan. Bring to a boil and reduce until mixture is like thick syrup. Strain and chill.

Combine berries and divide among 6 serving bowls. Top with a scoop of vanilla ice cream and spoon sauce over top.

Prep = 15 minutes   **Cook** = 30 to 35 minutes   **Yield** = 6 servings

Madeira Bread Pudding

Madeira is one of the most popular
fortified wines used in Colonial recipes. The inspiration
for this bread pudding comes from a dessert sampled at an
eighteenth-century tavern in Alexandria, Virginia.

- 4 large eggs
- 1 large egg yolk
- ¾ cup (150 g) sugar
- 1½ cups (355 ml) milk
- ½ cup (120 ml) Madeira wine
- 3 cups (710 ml) heavy (whipping) cream
- 1 teaspoon vanilla extract
- 1 teaspoon ground cinnamon
- ⅛ teaspoon grated nutmeg
- 1 loaf (12 ounces, or 340 g) French bread, cut into 1½-inch (3.8-cm) pieces (about 10 cups)
- ½ cup (75 g) golden raisins
- 2 tablespoons (28 g) butter, melted
- 2 tablespoons (26 g) sugar mixed with ½ teaspoon ground cinnamon

MADEIRA BUTTER SAUCE:
- 1 cup (200 g) sugar
- 2 tablespoons (16 g) cornstarch
- ½ cup (120 ml) light cream
- ¼ cup (60 ml) Madeira wine
- 1 teaspoon vanilla
- 1 stick (¼ pound, or 112 g) butter

Prep = 35 minutes **Cook** = 55 to 65 minutes **Yield** = 12 servings

Grease the bottom and sides of a 9 × 13-inch (22.5 × 32.5-cm) glass baking dish with nonstick cooking spray. In a large mixing bowl, beat eggs, egg yolk, ¾ cup (150 g) sugar, milk, Madeira, whipping cream, vanilla, cinnamon, and nutmeg with a wire whisk until well blended.

Stir in 7 cups (240 g) bread pieces and raisins. Allow to stand for 20 minutes. Preheat oven to 325°F (170°C, or gas mark 3). Pour into baking dish, Gently press remaining 3 cups (105 g) bread pieces on top of mixture in baking dish. Brush with melted butter and sprinkle with cinnamon mixture. Bake for 55 to 65 minutes until puffy and light golden brown (center should still jiggle slightly). Cool 30 minutes before serving with warm Madeira Butter Sauce.

For Madeira Butter Sauce: Combine sugar and cornstarch in a medium saucepan. Blend in light cream, Madeira, and vanilla. Add butter and bring to a boil, stirring constantly, until slightly thickened.

Port Wine
Pecan Pie

It seems like everyone sneaks a little bourbon into their pecan pies. An equally delectable substitution is port wine.

- 4 tablespoons (55 g) butter
- 1 cup (225 g) firmly packed brown sugar
- 1 cup (340 g) dark corn syrup
- ¼ cup (60 ml) port wine
- 1 teaspoon vanilla extract
- ¼ teaspoon salt
- 4 eggs, beaten
- 1 ¼ cups (138 g) toasted pecans*

Combine butter, sugar, corn syrup, and port in a medium saucepan. Cook, stirring constantly, over low heat until sugar dissolves and mixture bubbles. Remove from heat and cool for 10 minutes.

Meanwhile, preheat the oven to 325°F (170°C, or gas mark 3). Beat vanilla, salt, and eggs into sugar mixture. Stir in pecans and pour into pie shell that has been set on a baking sheet. Place on the lowest rack in the oven. Bake for 50 to 55 minutes. Allow to cool to room temperature before slicing.

*To toast pecans: Preheat oven to 350°F (180°C, or gas mark 4) and spread pecans on a baking sheet. Bake for 6 to 8 minutes, stirring once or twice, until evenly golden brown. Watch carefully to avoid burning.

Prep = 20 minutes   **Cook** = 60 to 65 minutes
Yield = 8 to 10 servings

Peach and Champagne Sorbet

Experimenting with an ice-cream maker will soon show that alcohol affects how hard the mixture in the canister will freeze. Many alcohol-infused ice cream recipes simply come out too soft to be scooped. Fresh fruit sorbets have a tendency to freeze very hard, so the alcohol in Champagne is advantageous in a recipe such as this.

1½ pounds (680 g) fresh, ripe freestone peaches
½   cup (100 g) plus 1 tablespoon (13 g) sugar
½   cup (120 ml) water
1   tablespoon (6 g) grated lemon zest
¾   cup (175 ml) Champagne

Place peaches in a large saucepan and cover with boiling water. Return to a boil and cook for 2 minutes. Drain and rinse in cold water. Peel peaches, halve them, and remove pits. Place peaches in a food processor and purée. In a small saucepan, bring sugar, water, and lemon zest to a boil and simmer for 3 minutes. Remove from heat and let stand for at least 10 minutes. Combine sugar syrup with Champagne and peaches.

Chill mixture for at least 4 hours. Transfer to an ice-cream freezer and freeze according to manufacturer's directions.

Prep = 30 minutes **Cook** = 10 minutes
Chill = 4 hours **Yield** = 1 quart

Port-Poached
Pears Glacé

There's a simple elegance to poached pears
for dessert. They are also suitable as a garnish for poultry
and side dishes. They are easy to prepare ahead of
time for a dinner party and are a light ending
to a heavy meal.

- 6   ripe pears
- 1   cup (240 ml) port wine
- 1   cup (240 ml) orange juice
- ½   cup (100 g) sugar
- 1   teaspoon vanilla extract
- 1   orange
- 1   quart (945 ml) vanilla ice cream

Peel pears and core from the bottom, leaving stem intact at
the top. Combine port, orange juice, sugar, and vanilla in a large
saucepan. Cut skin of orange into julienne strips and add to
saucepan along with pears.

Bring to a boil, cover, and simmer for 10 to 15 minutes or until
pears are tender (Do not overcook). Remove pears and simmer
liquid for an additional 15 minutes or until reduced by two-thirds.
Chill pears in syrup. Serve each pear with a scoop of vanilla ice
cream.

Prep = 15 minutes   **Cook** = 30 to 35 minutes
Yield = 6 servings

Sweet Potato Pie
with Sherry

Usually, bourbon is the spirit of choice in sweet potato pie. Spiking it with a little sherry works the same magic. Unlike pumpkin pie, this dessert is in season at a summer barbecue as well as Thanksgiving dinner.

- 3 sweet potatoes, about 8 ounces (225 g) each
- 4 tablespoons (55 g) butter, melted
- ⅓ cup (80 ml) half-and-half
- ⅓ cup (67 g) firmly packed light brown sugar
- ⅓ cup (80 ml) maple syrup
- 3 large eggs, beaten
- ¼ cup (60 ml) sherry
- 1 teaspoon vanilla extract
- ¼ teaspoon ground cinnamon
- ¼ teaspoon grated nutmeg
- ¼ teaspoon salt
- 1 unbaked pie shell, 9 inches (22.5-cm)

Preheat oven temperature to 425°F (220°C, or gas mark 7). Roast sweet potatoes in oven for about an hour or until they are easily pierced with a fork. Cool to room temperature and remove peels. Put sweet potatoes in a large mixing bowl and mash with a potato masher until smooth.

Reduce oven temperature to 350°F (180°C, or gas mark 4). Add butter, half-and-half, brown sugar, maple syrup, eggs, sherry, vanilla, cinnamon, nutmeg, and salt to sweet potatoes and blend until smooth with a wire whisk. Pour into pie shell that has been placed on a baking sheet. Set pie on the lowest oven rack and bake for about 50 minutes, or until a knife inserted in the center comes out clean. Cool completely before slicing.

Prep = 30 minutes   **Cook** = 1¾ hours   **Yield** = 8 servings

Index

About the Author

Alison Boteler is the author of nine books. She is a newspaper columnist and magazine contributor whose credits include the *Connecticut Post*, *Fairfield County Weekly*, and *Family Fun* magazine. Her career began at an early age with cooking spots for kids on WNEW's *Wonderama* and regular appearances on *Midday Live with Bill Boggs* in New York City. While in college, she hosted her own radio show, *Alison's Restaurant*, on WCWP FM and had Julia Child as one of her first guests. After graduation, she made appearances on NBC's *Today Show* and later became a regular on Lifetime's *Our Home*. She has been a creative consultant to several major food companies. Alison lives in Connecticut.

Acknowledgments

I'd like to give a special thanks to Lee Steele and Bill Boteler for their editorial contribution to this book.

No book is created without a little help from your friends. I want to thank the following people for their recipes, taste testing, and support during this project: Paul Arroyo, Lisa and John O'Brien, Marc Chebbi, James Comstock, Mary Beth Doughty, Franco Grimaldi, Diane Jacobsen, Rod and B.C. Molinare, and Charlotte Mueller.